Pop Art Raketen

Eckhard Schmittner

IMPRESSUM

© 2018, Eckhard Schmittner

Titel: Pop Art Raketen

Alle Rechte vorbehalten.

Coverbild: Bettina Bauch

Covergestaltung: Bettina Bauch

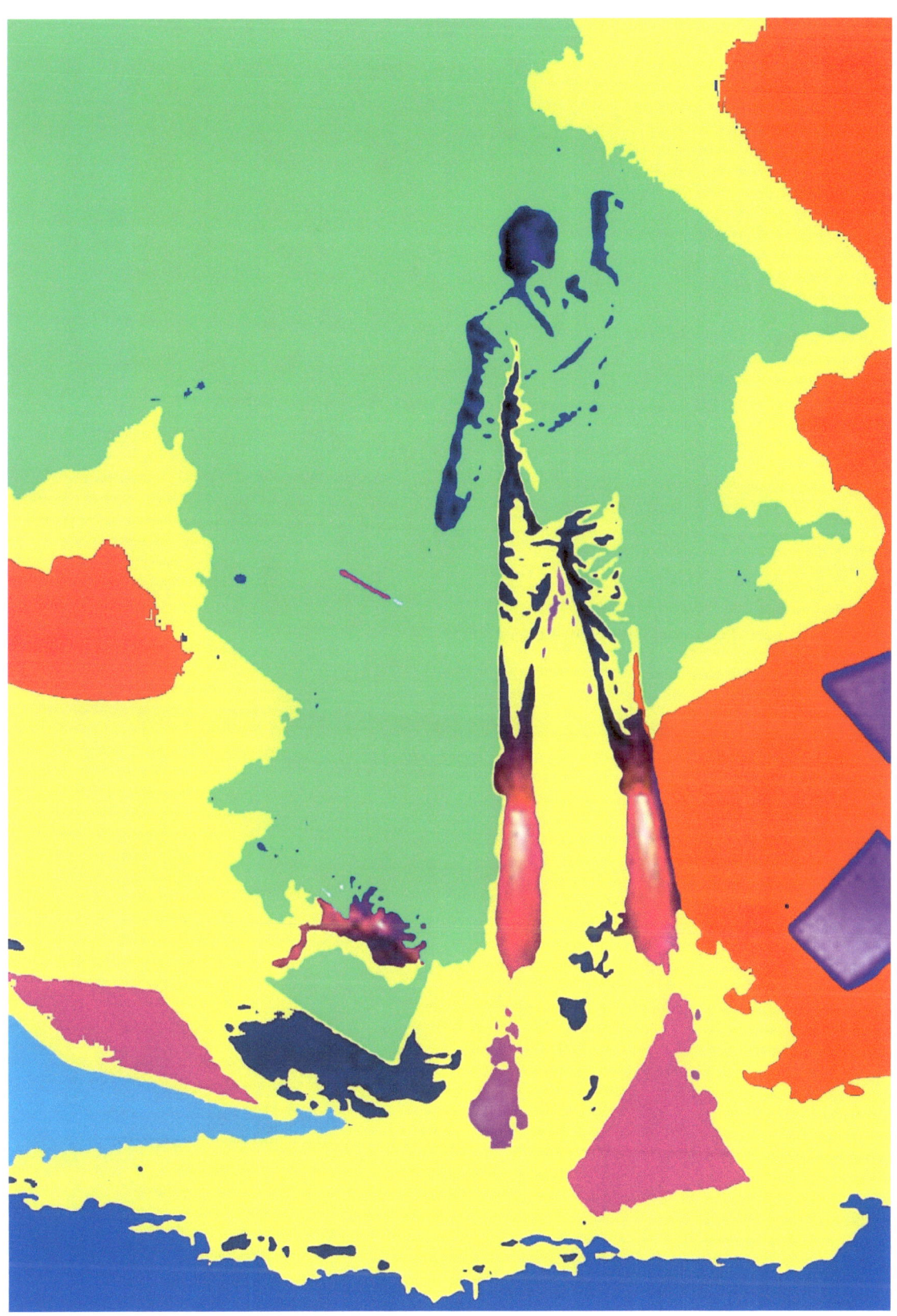

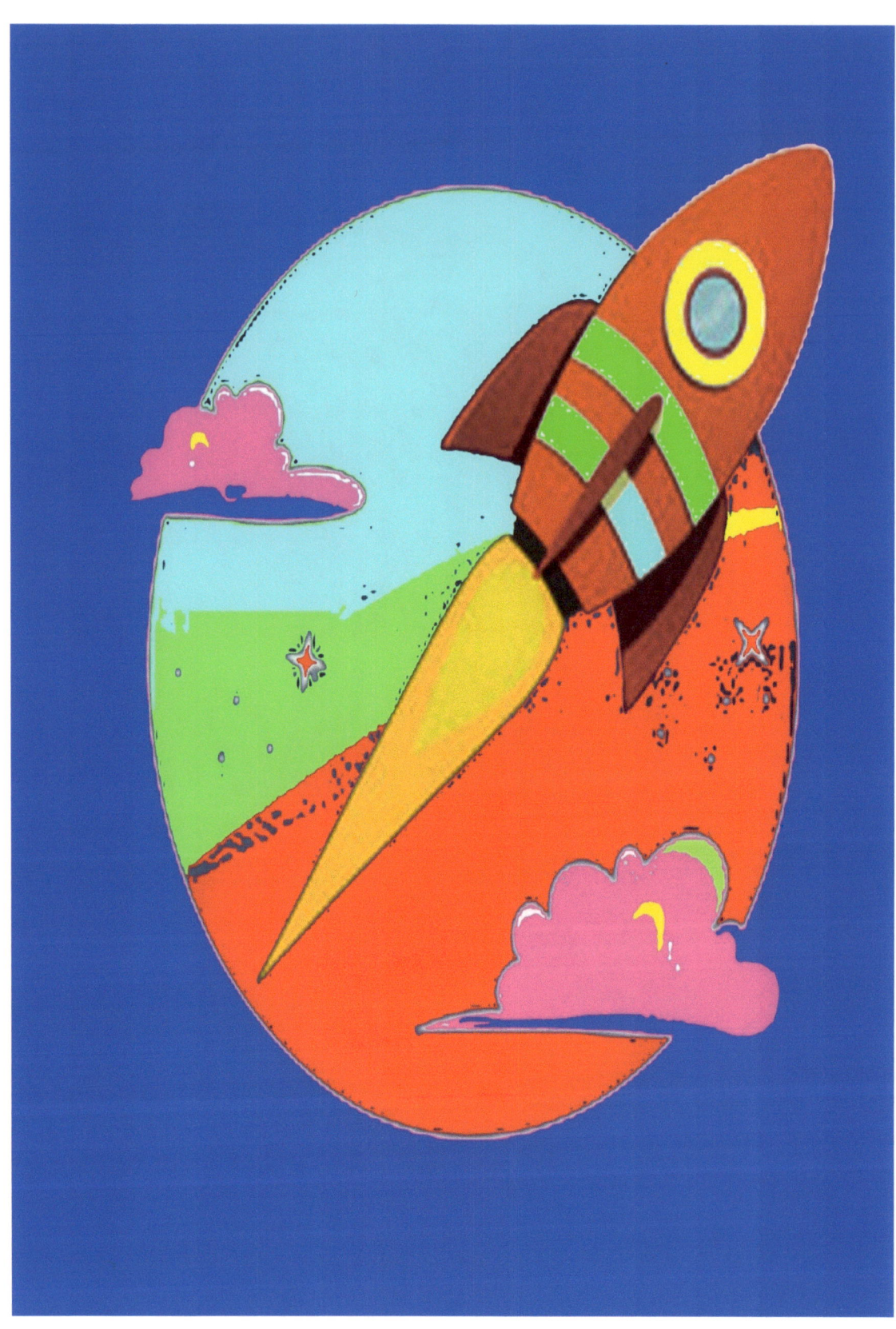

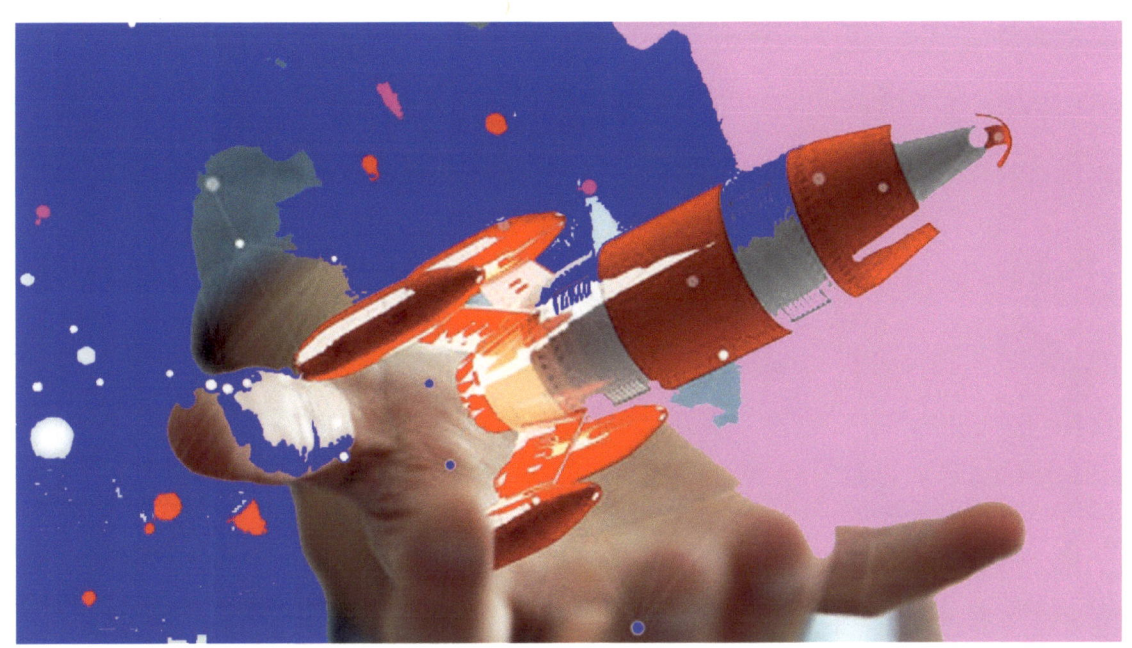

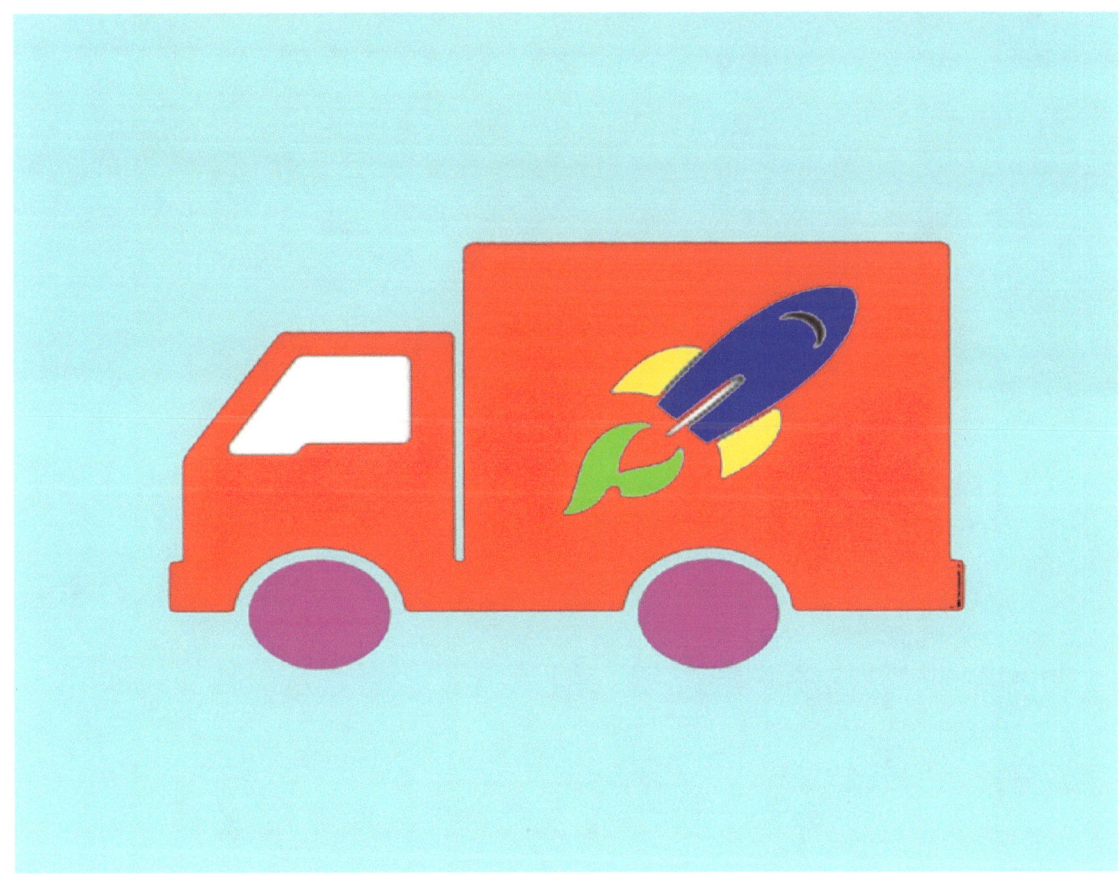

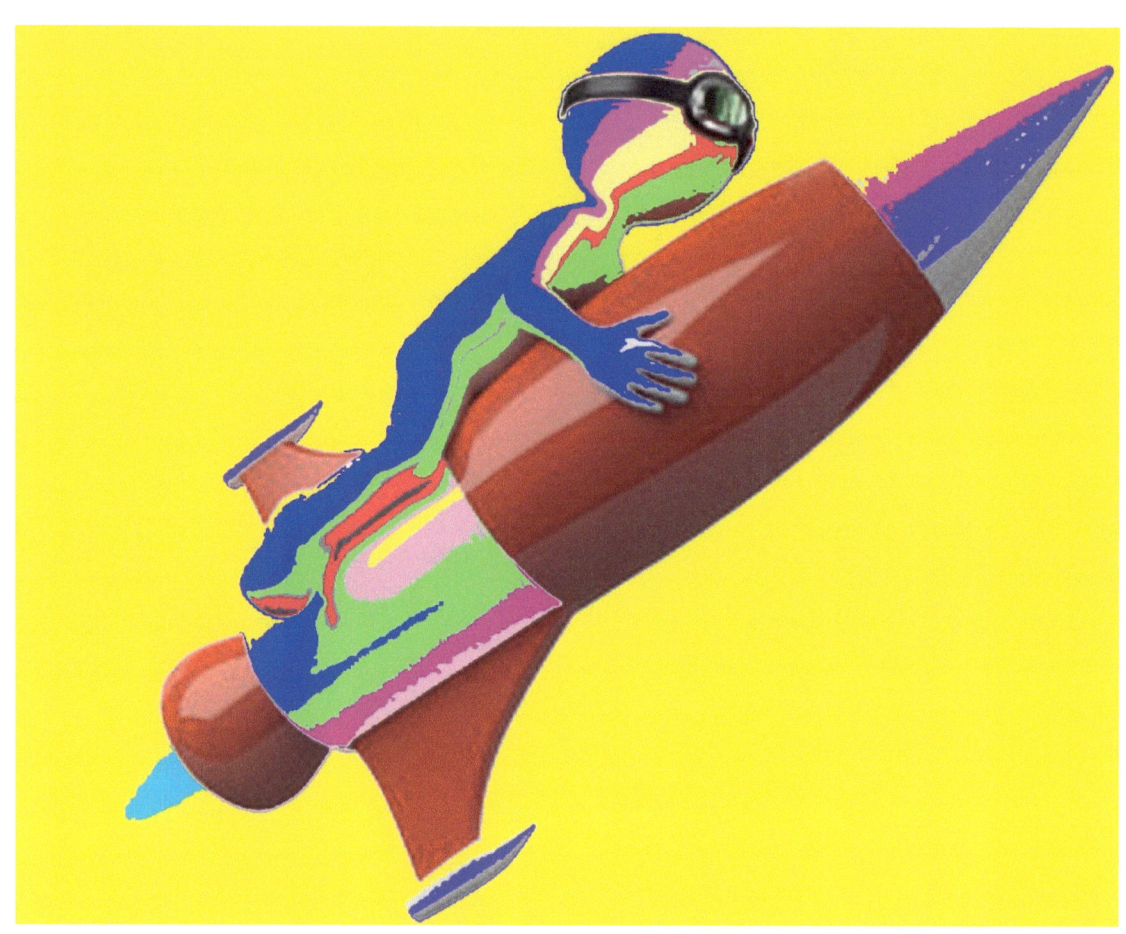
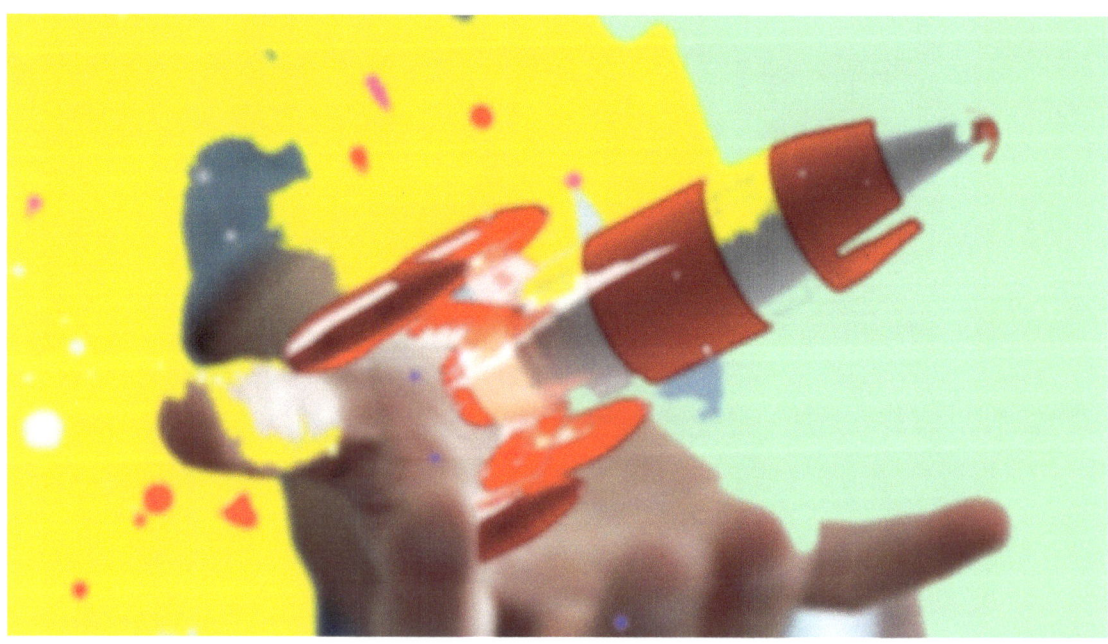

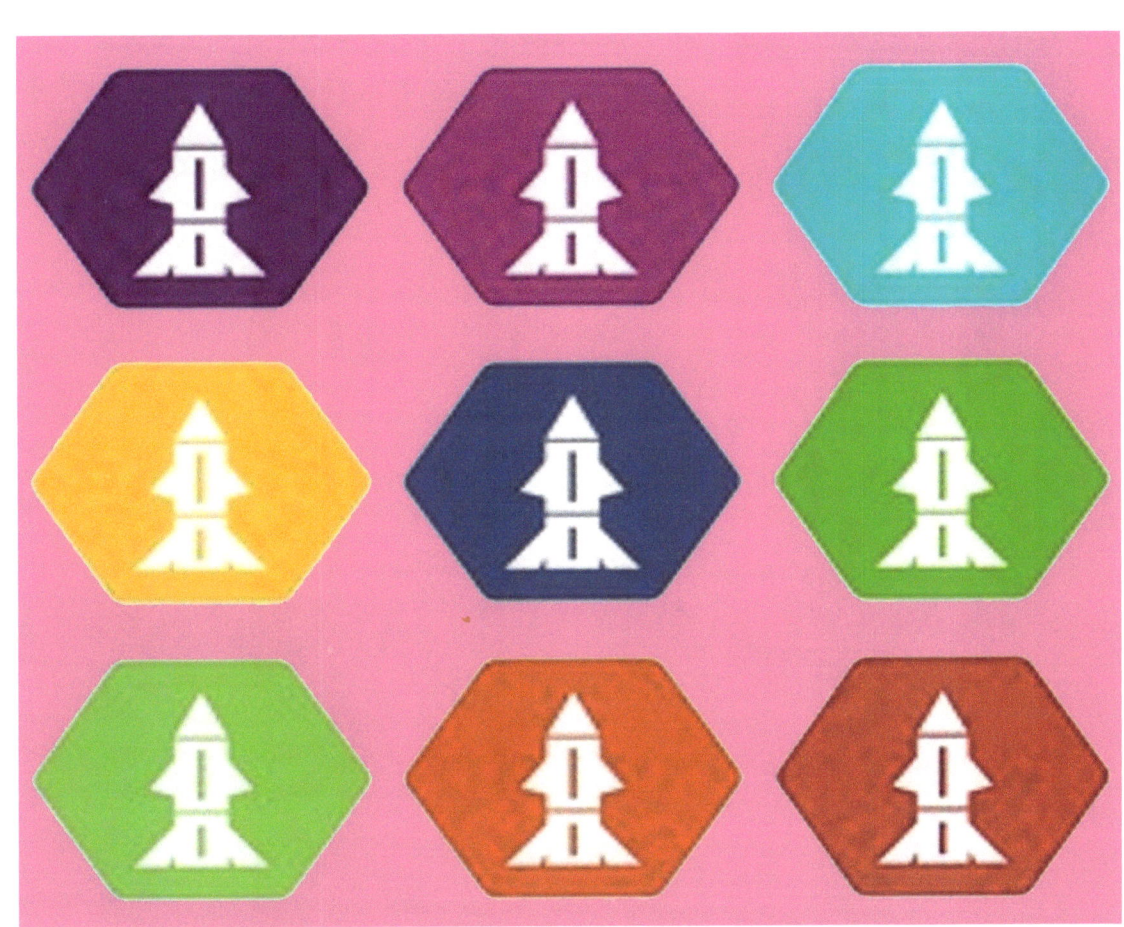
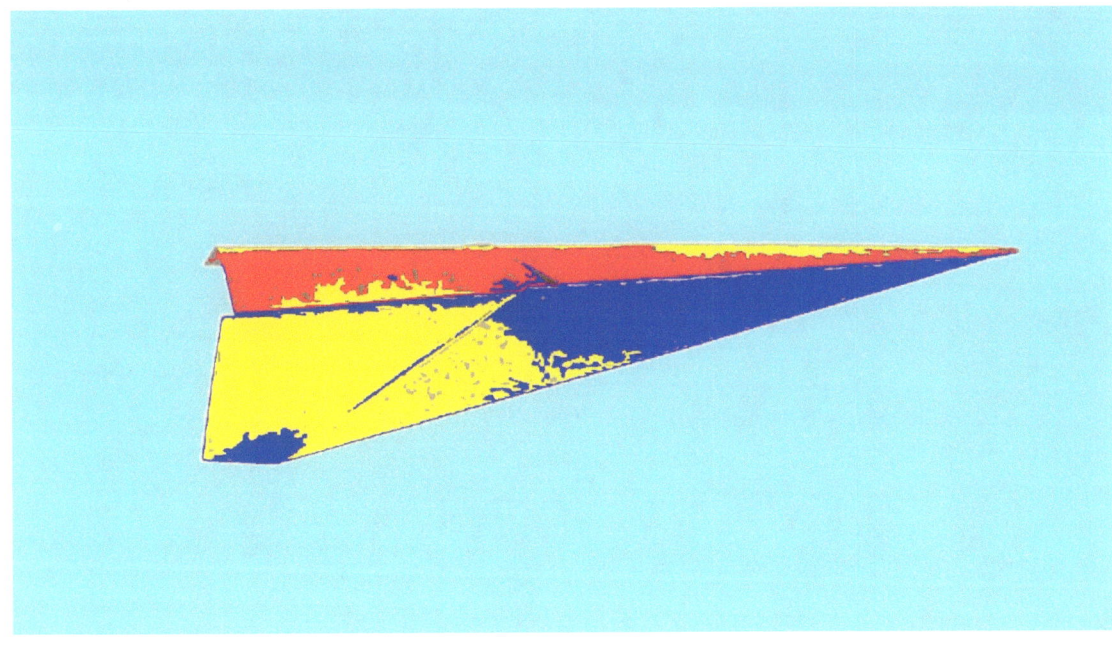

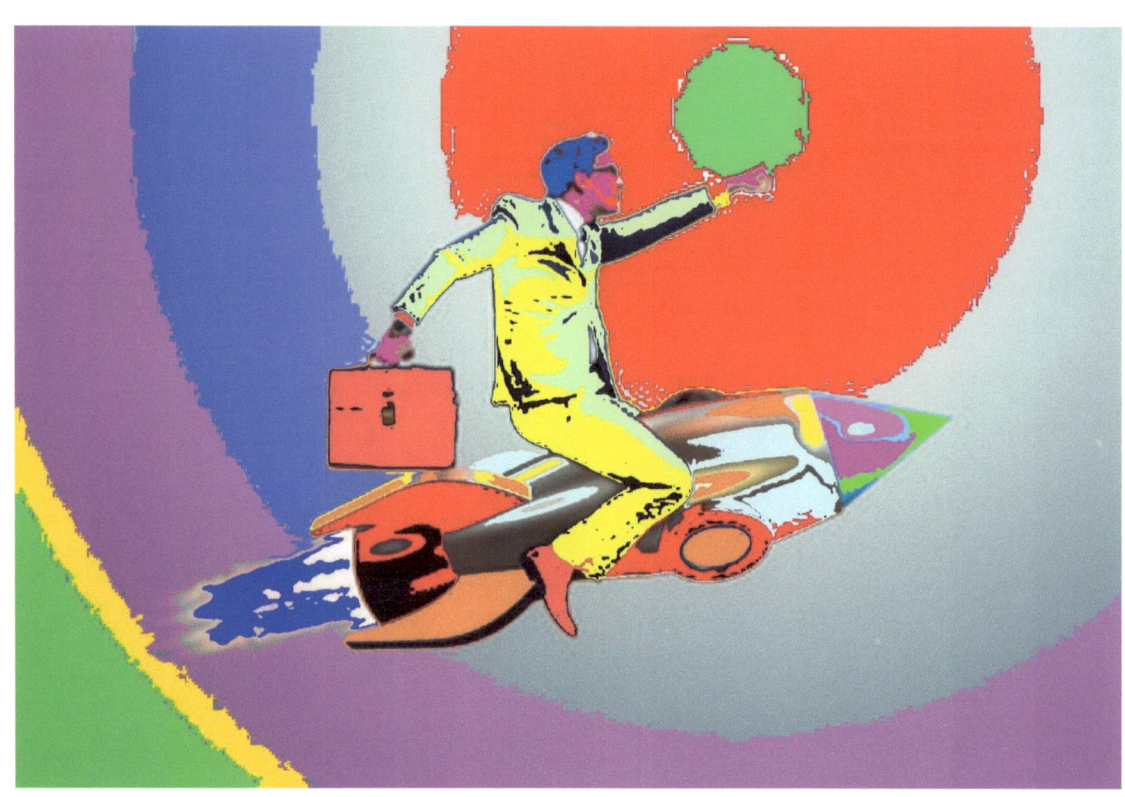
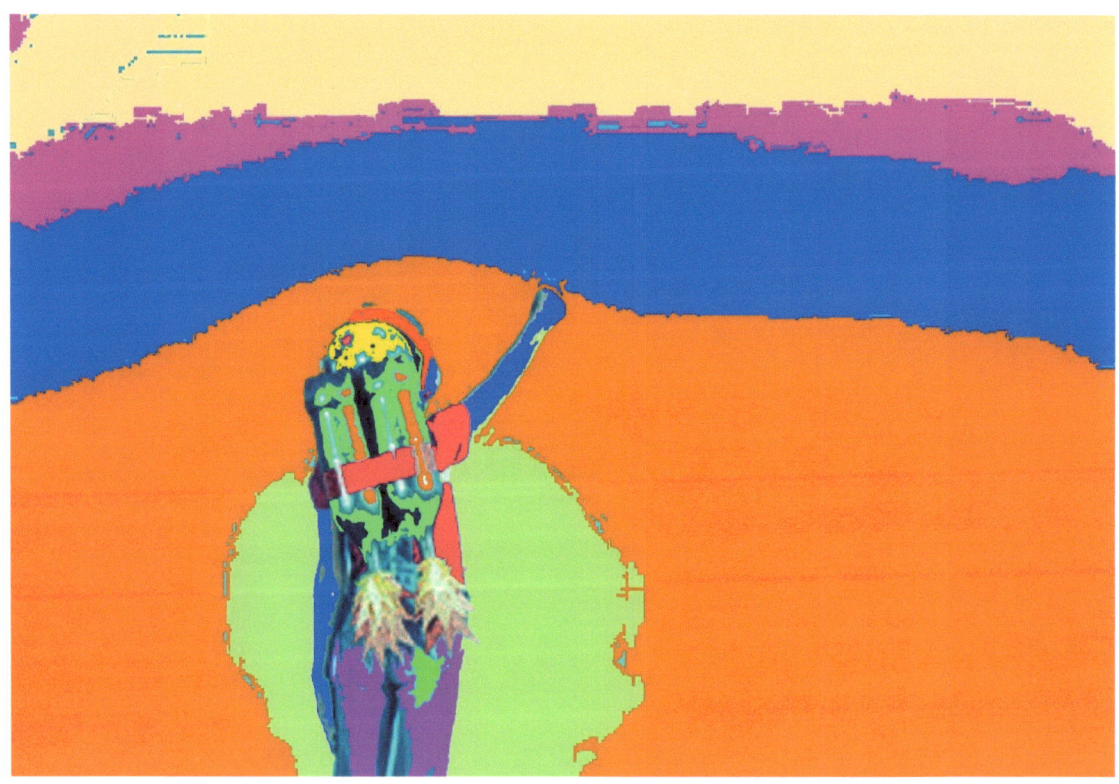

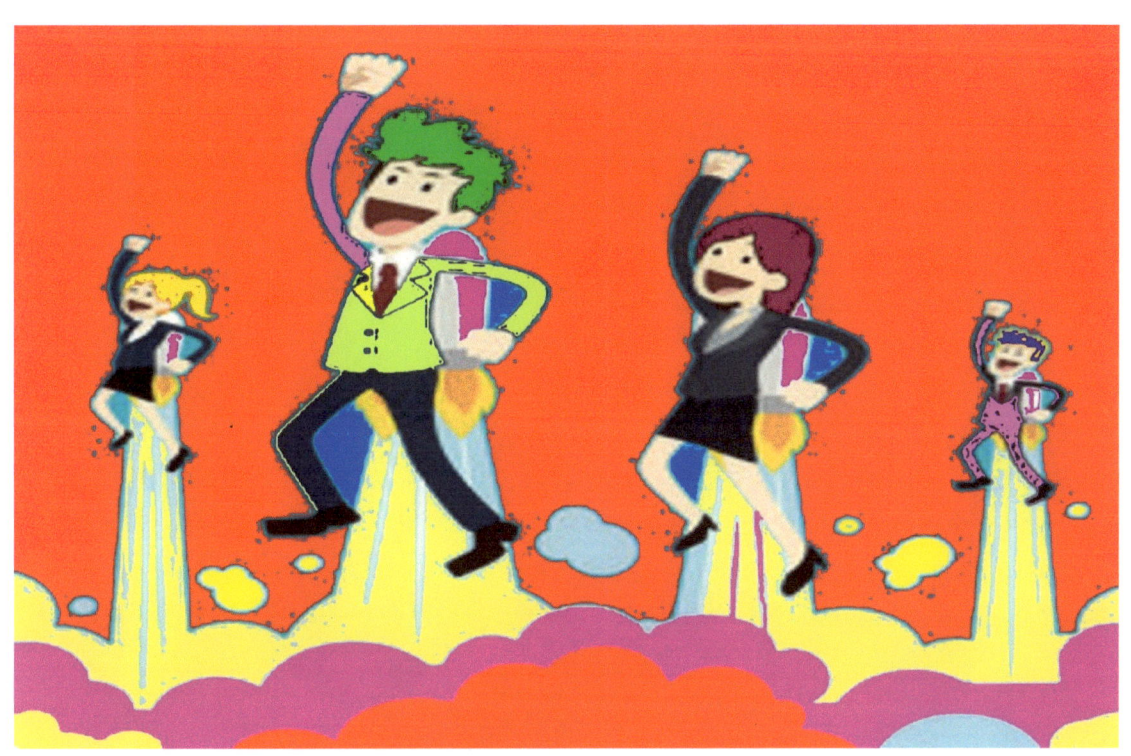

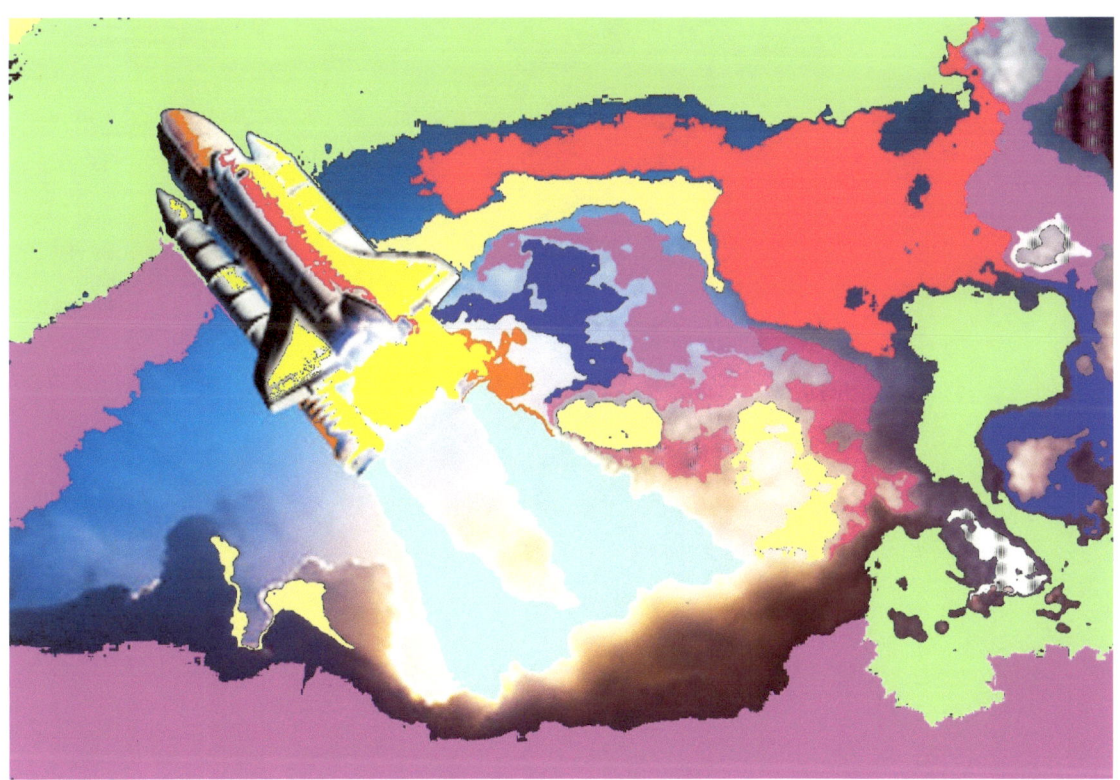

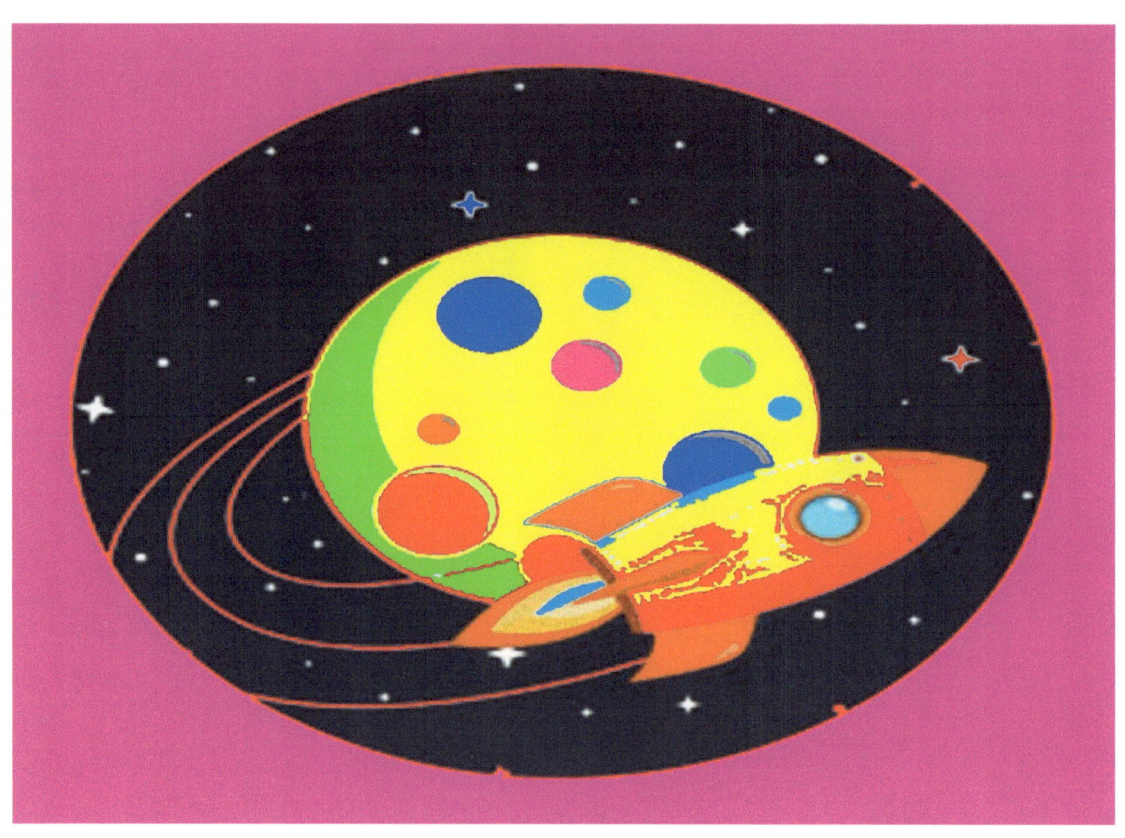

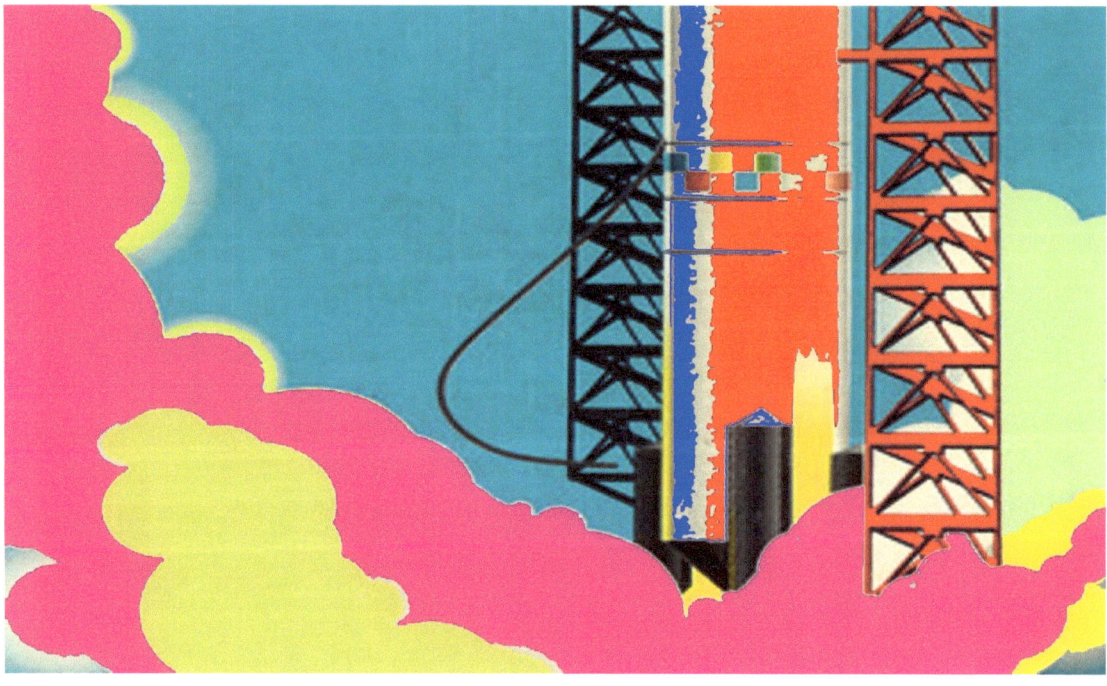

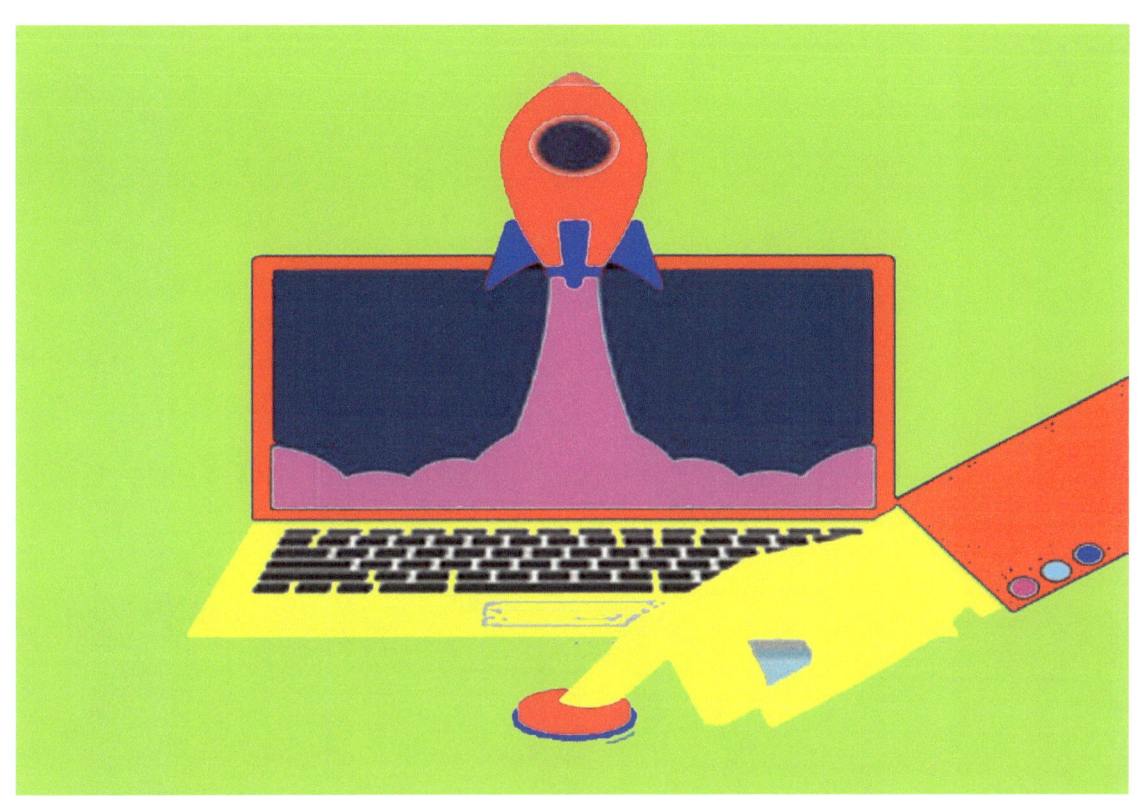

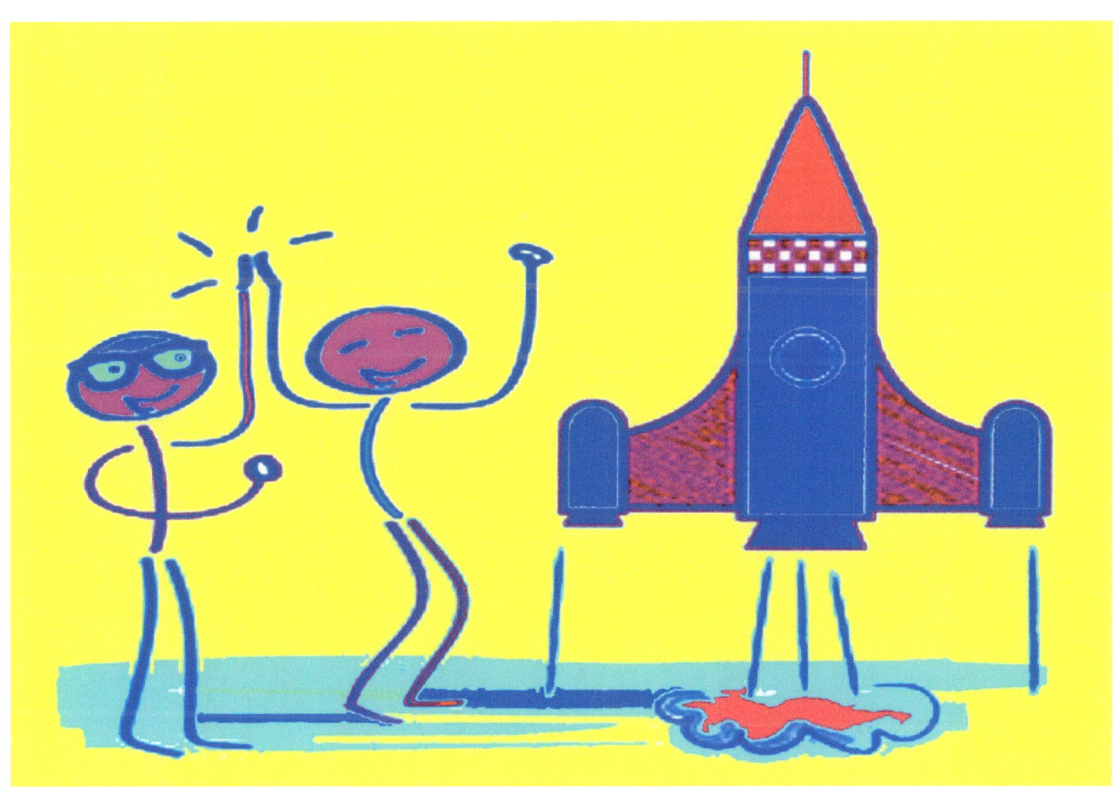

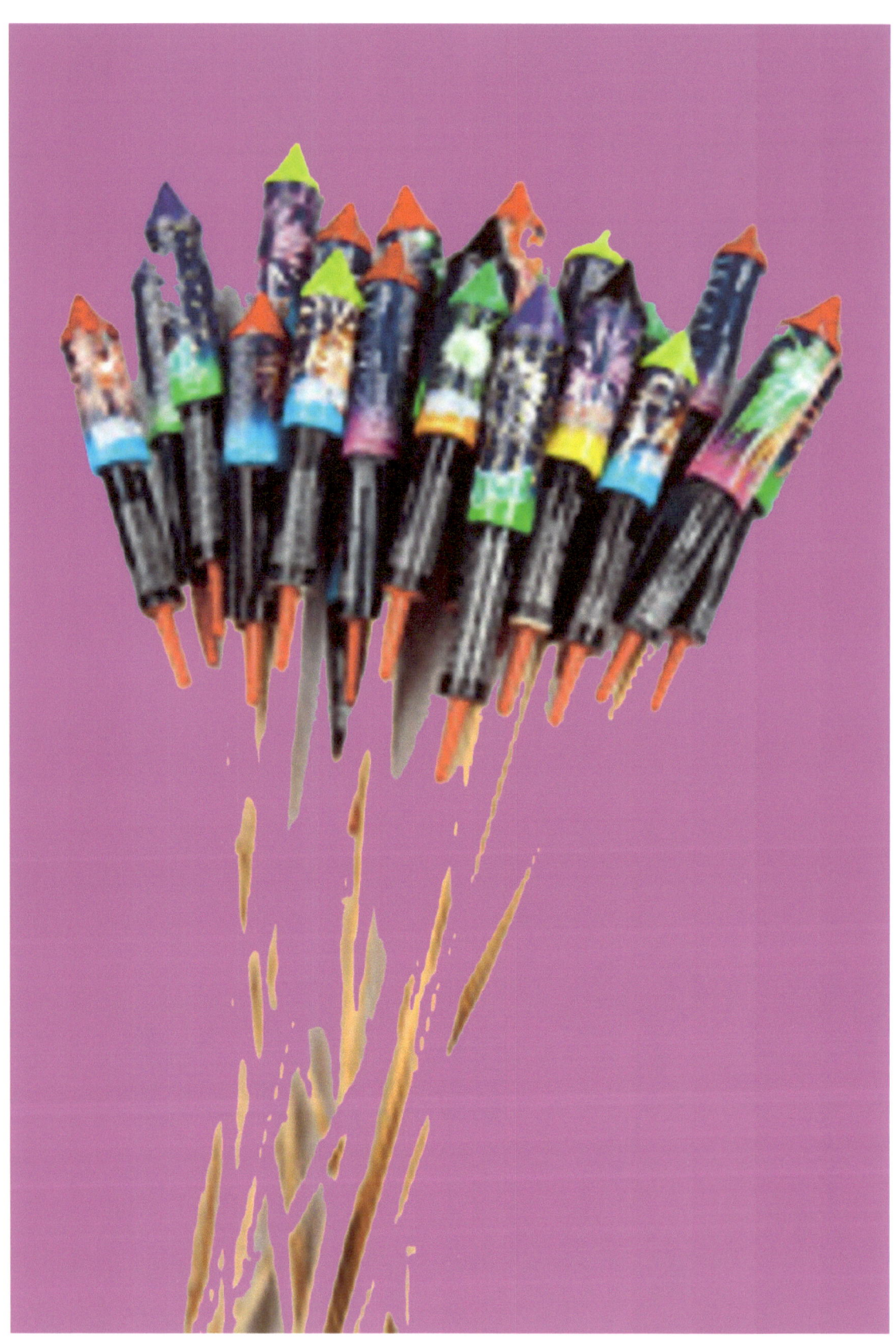

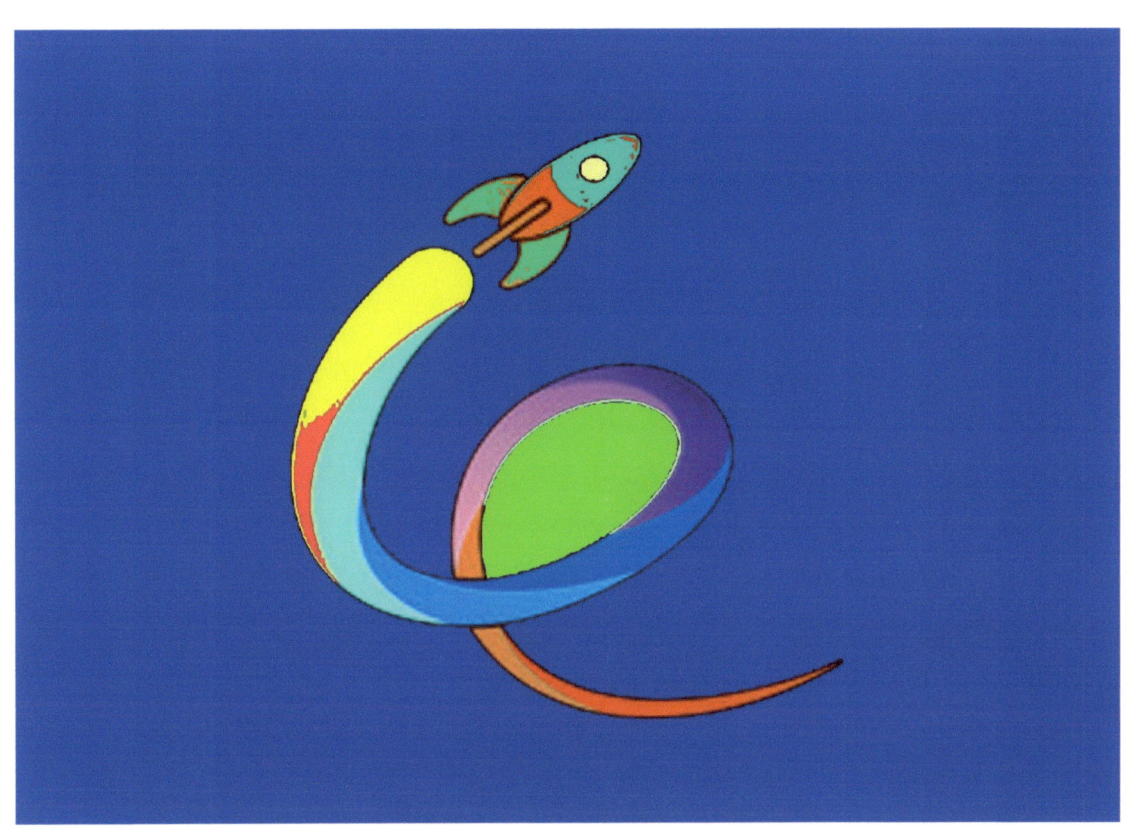

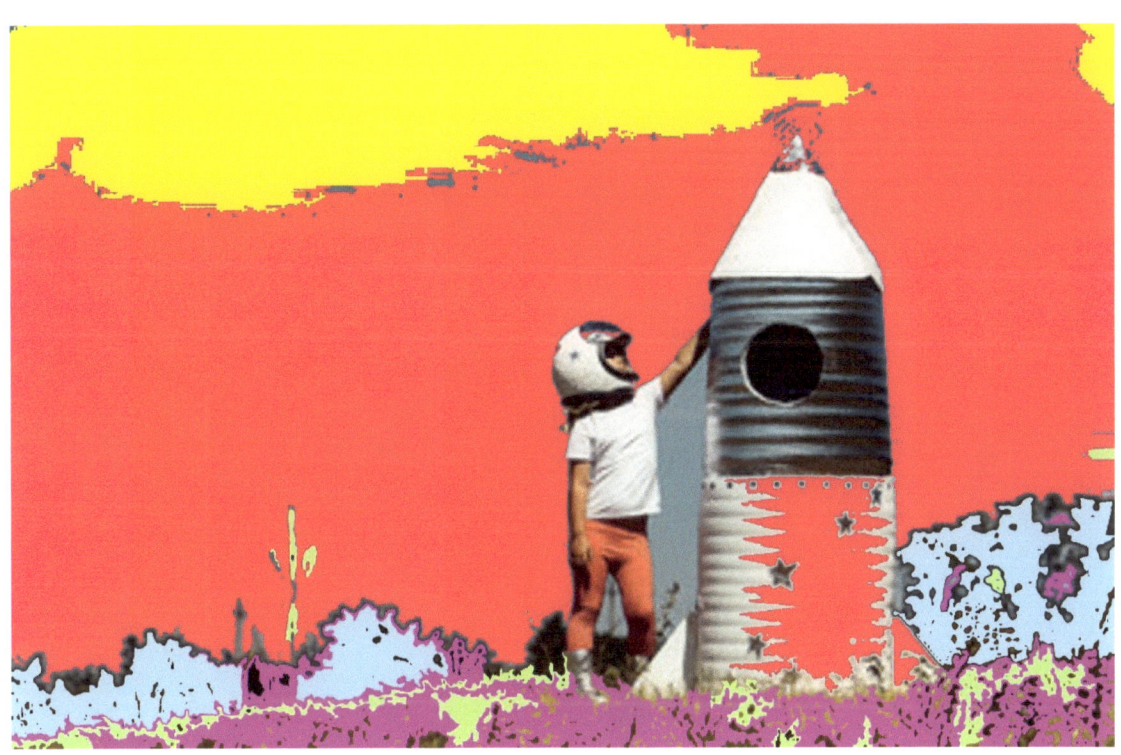

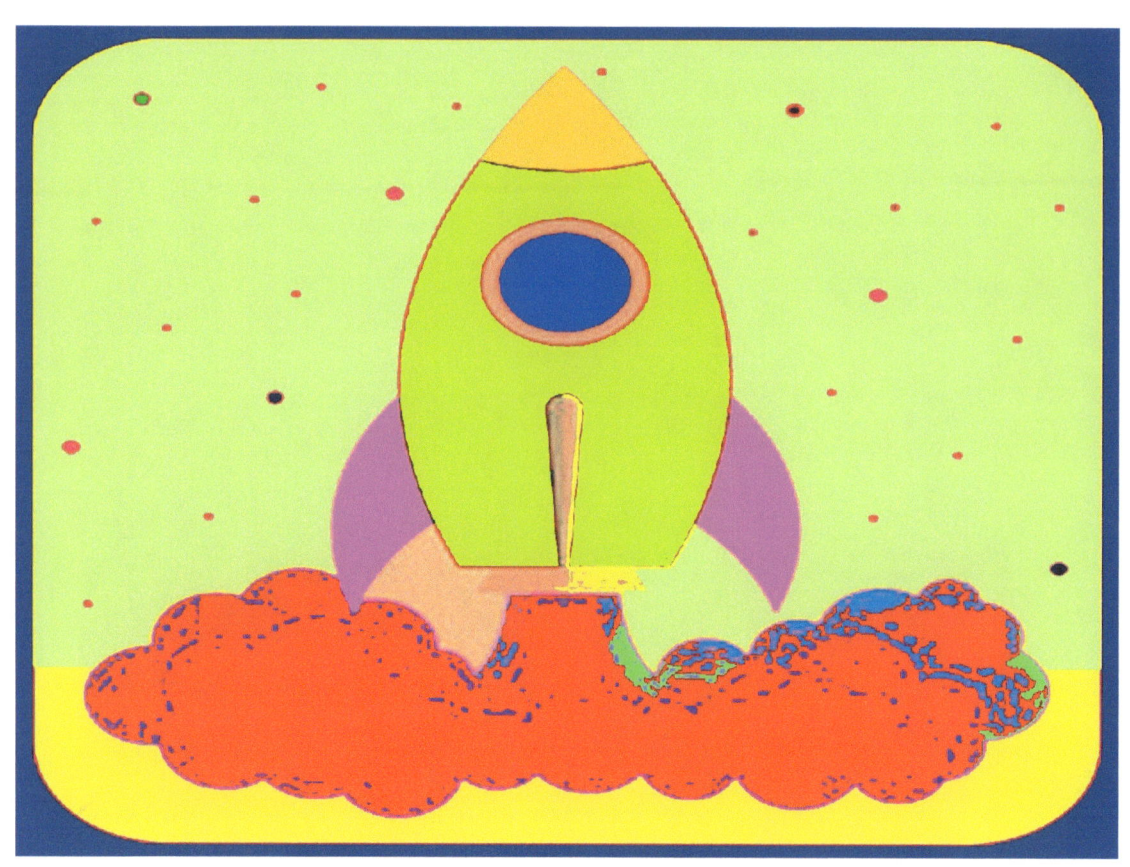
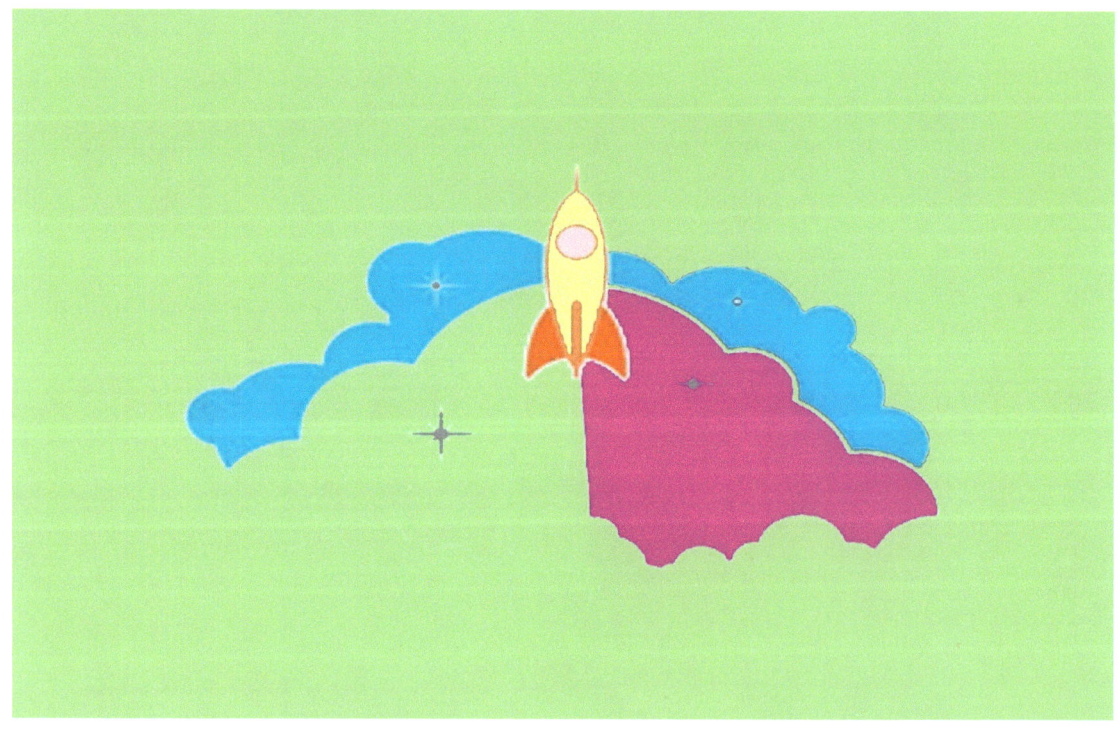

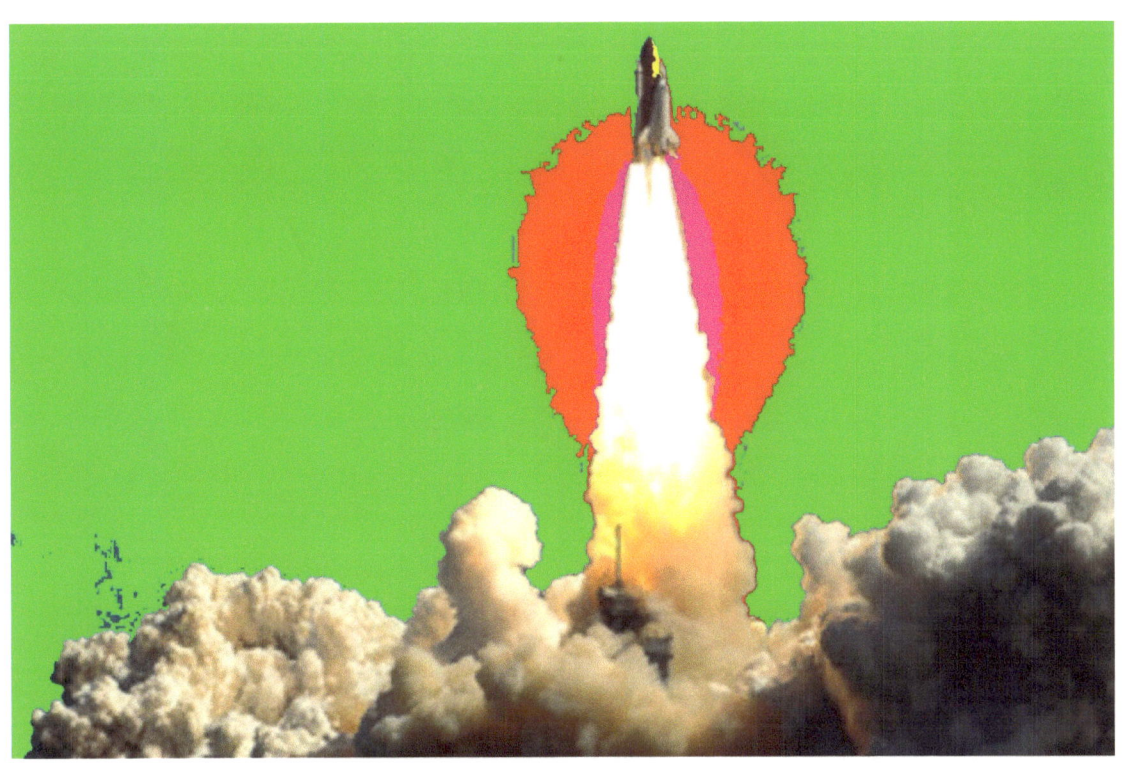
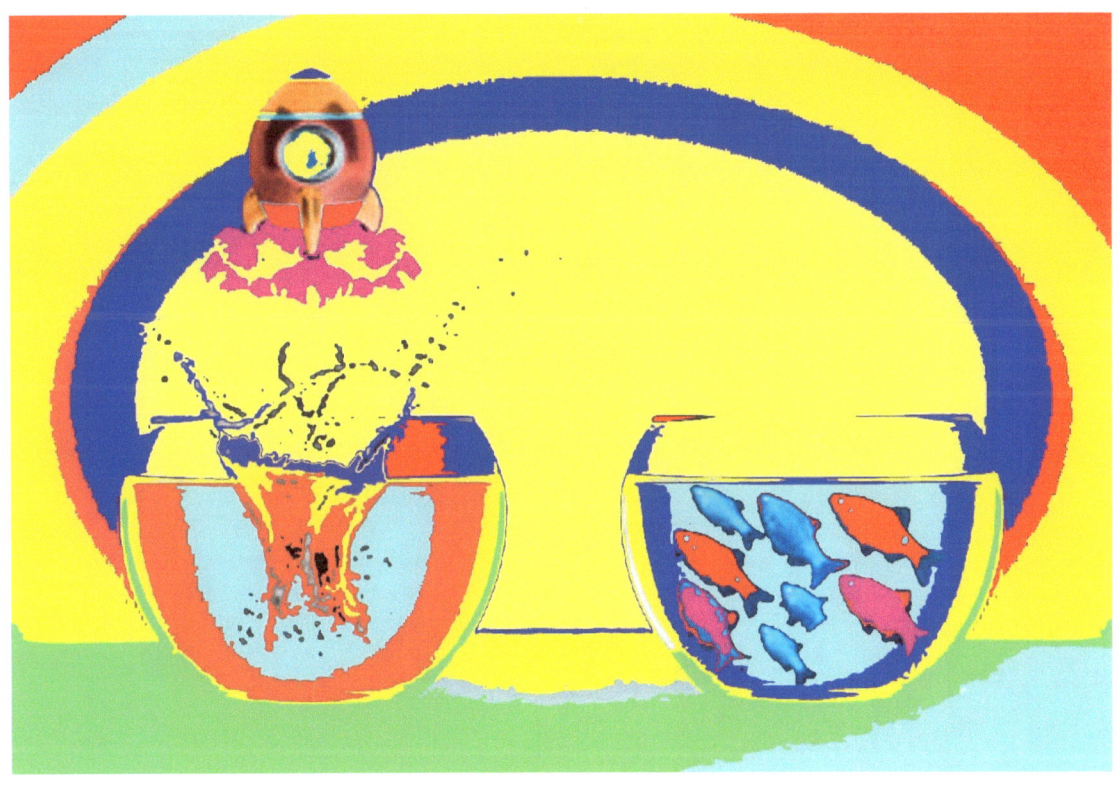

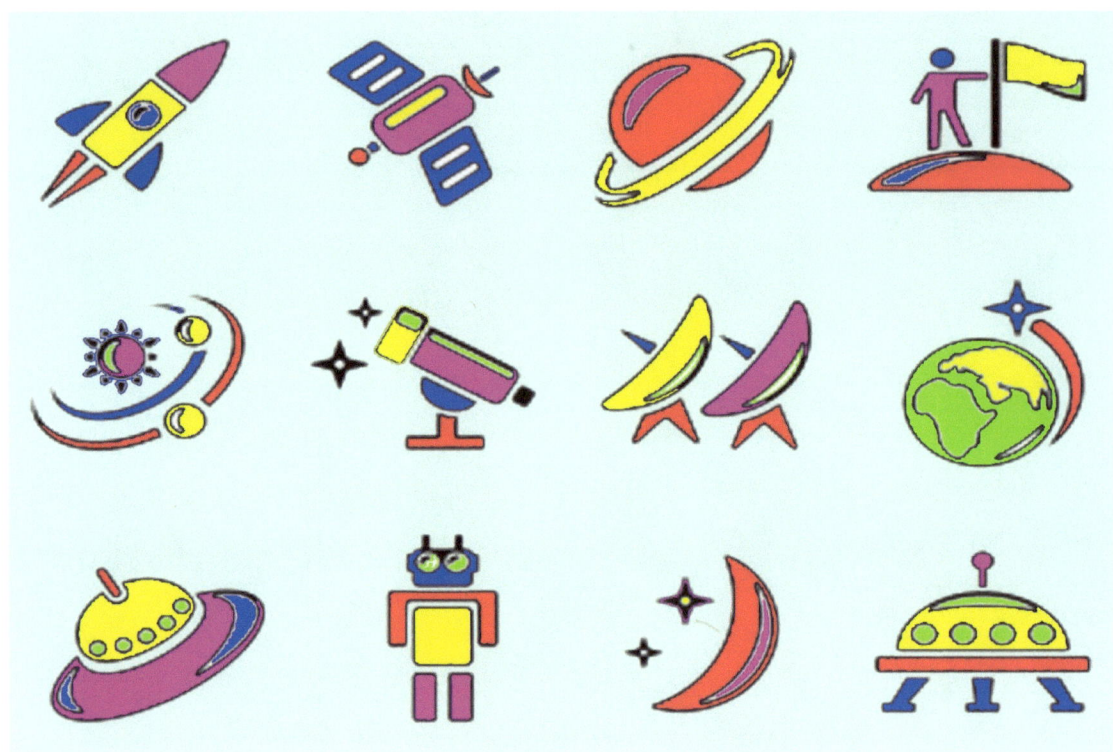
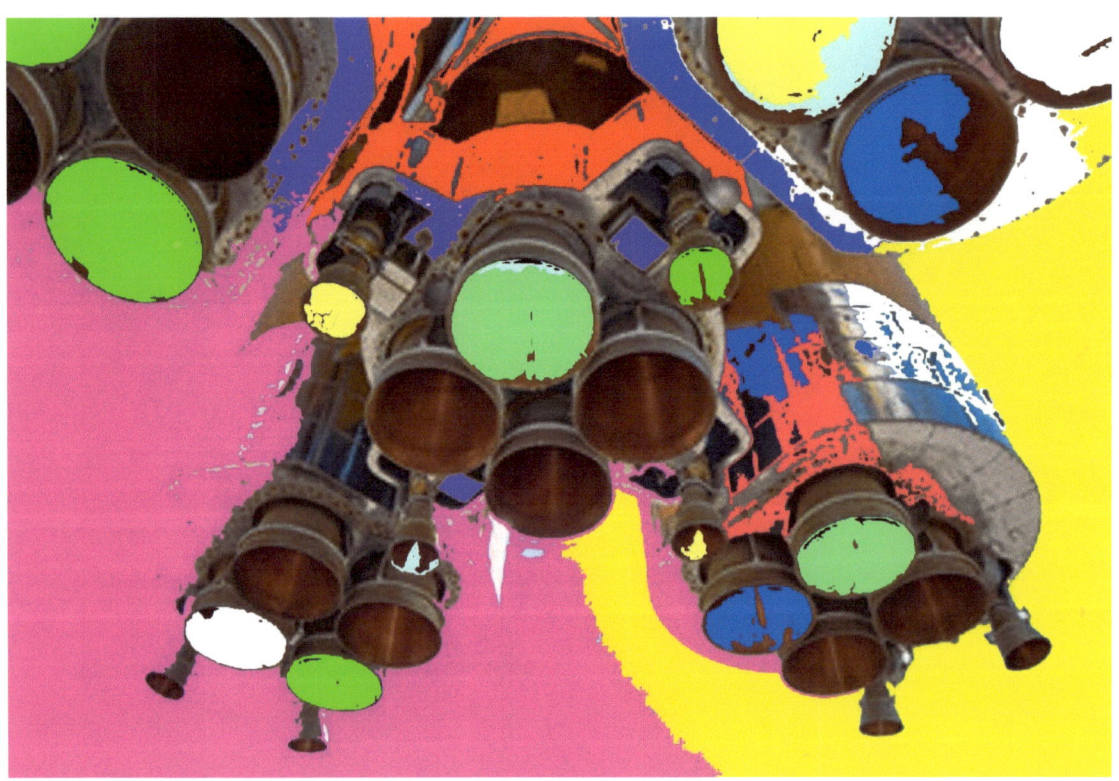

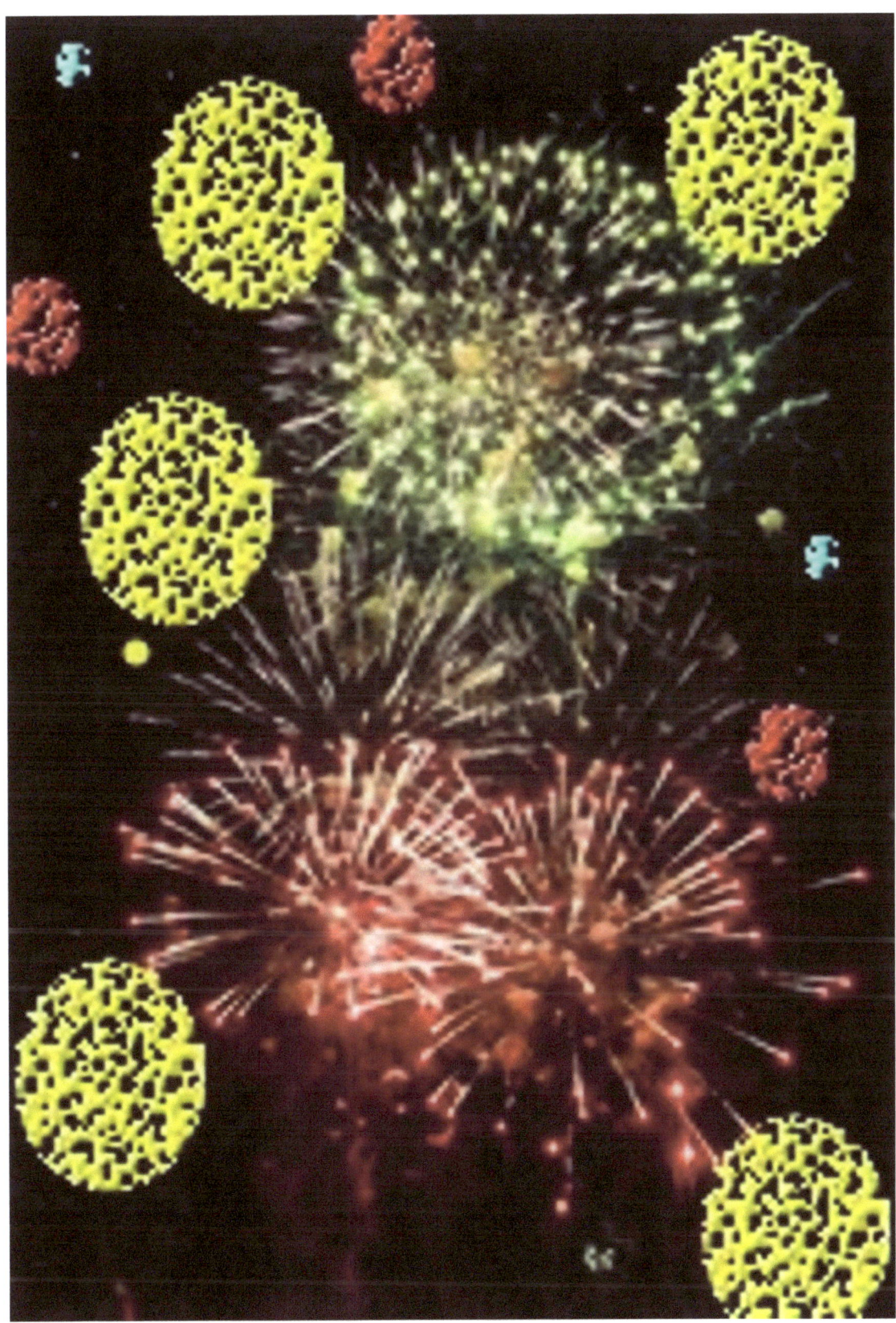

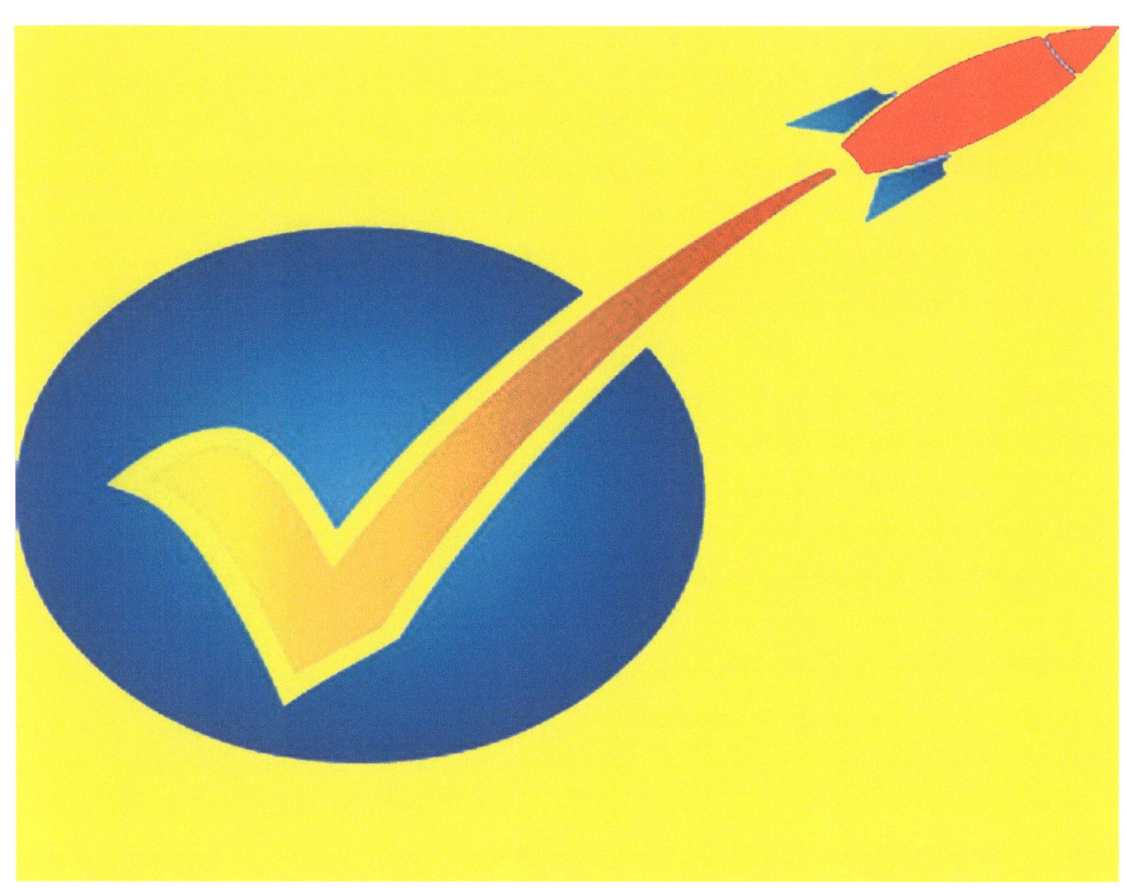
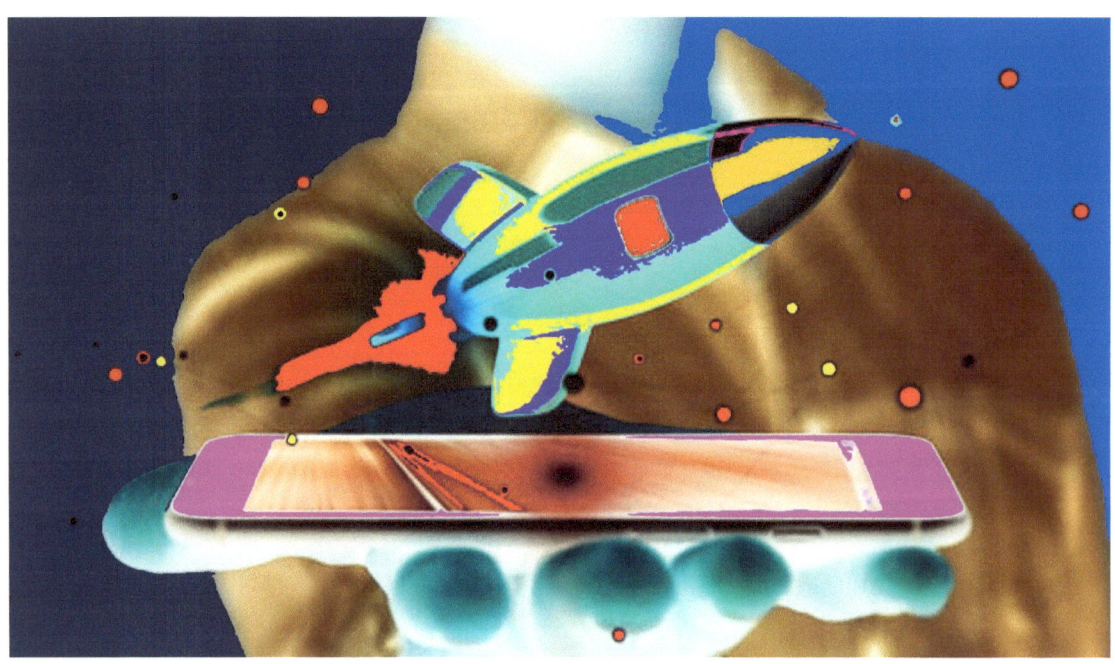

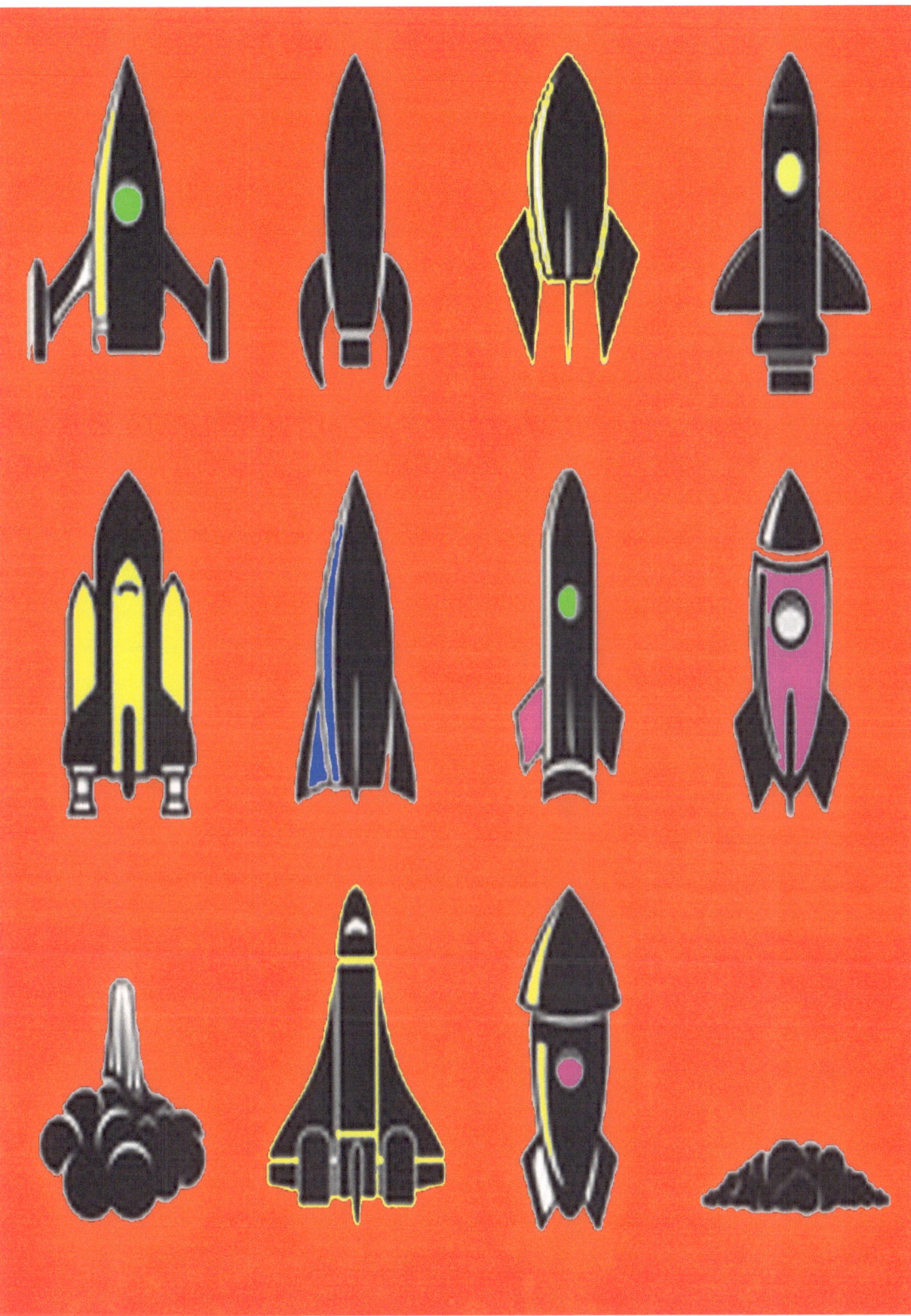

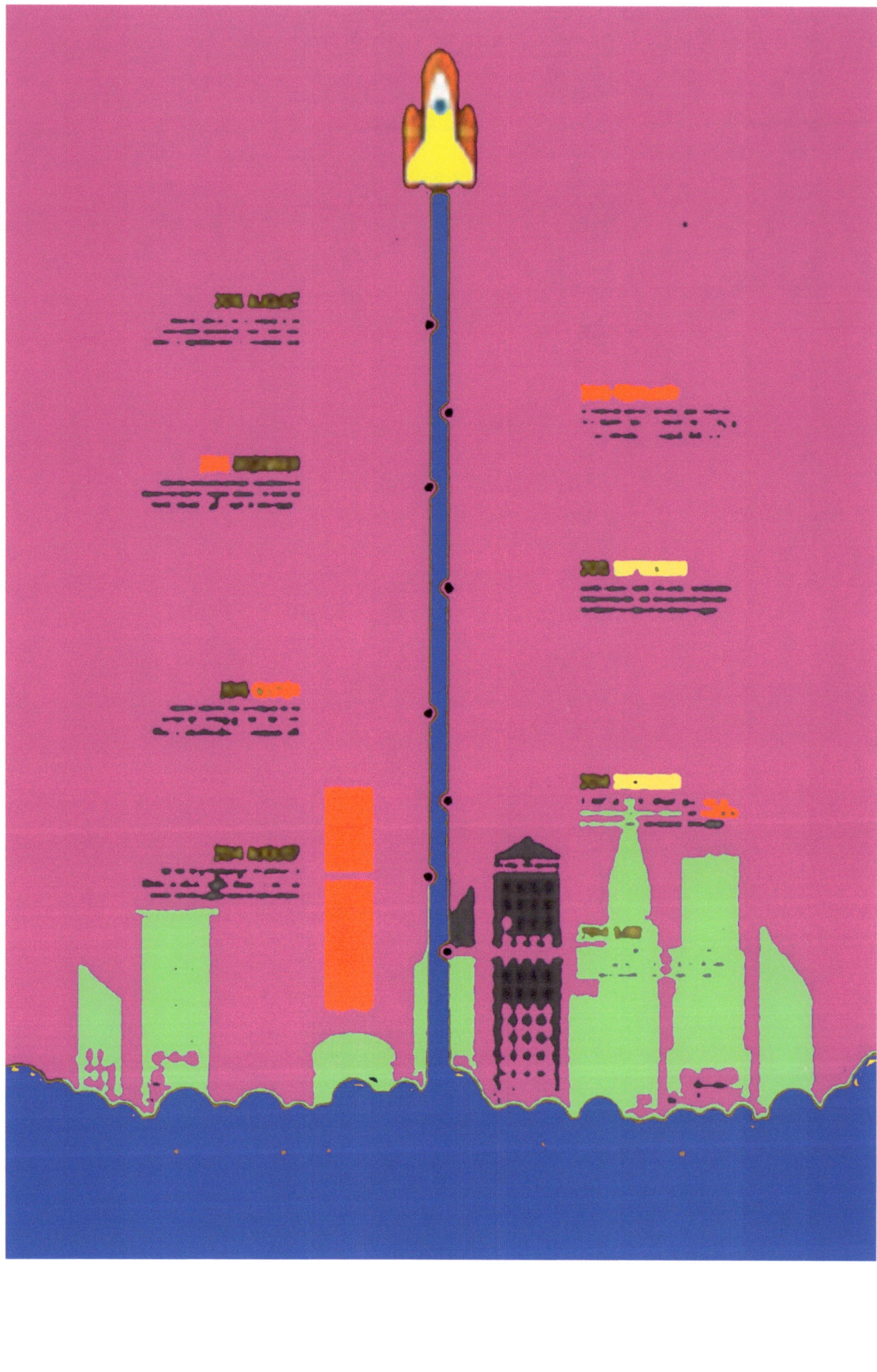

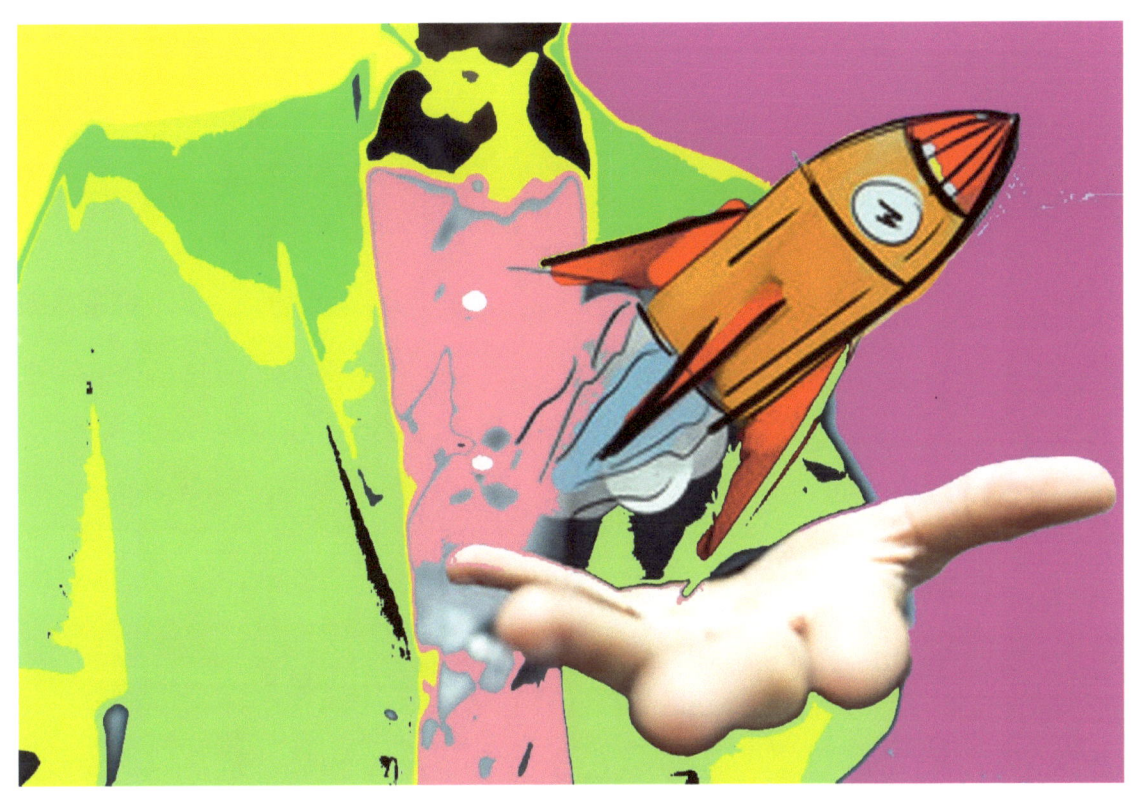
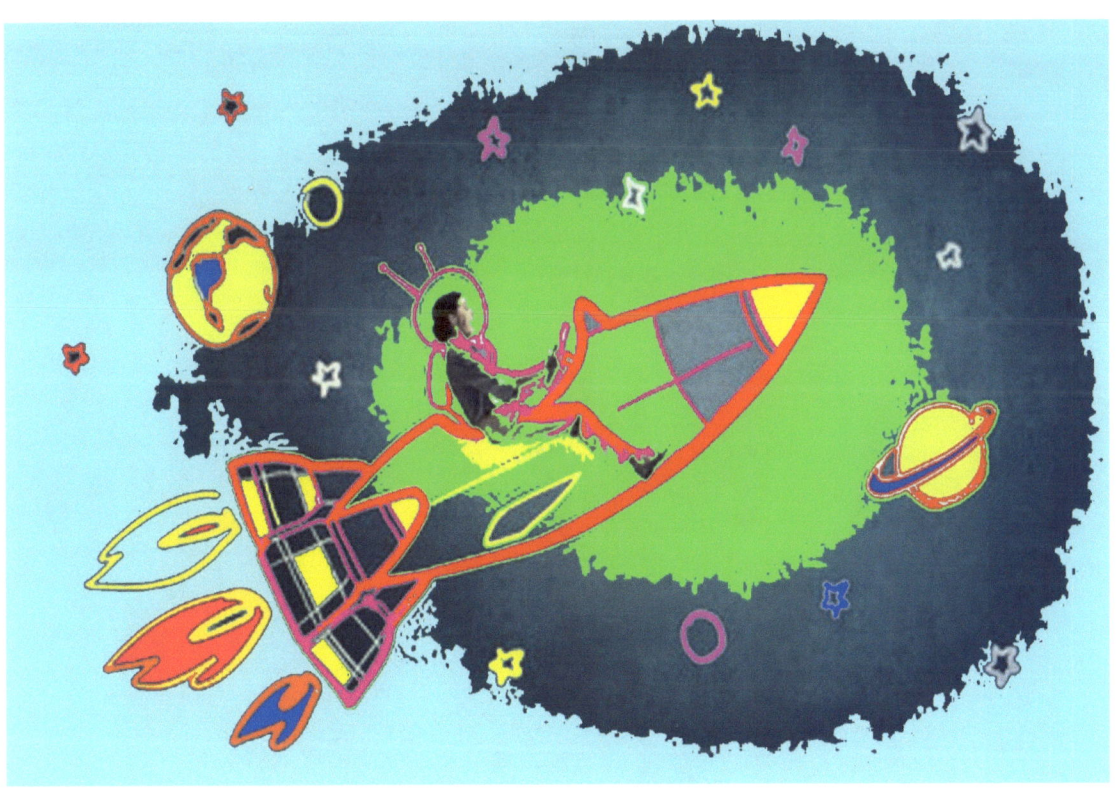

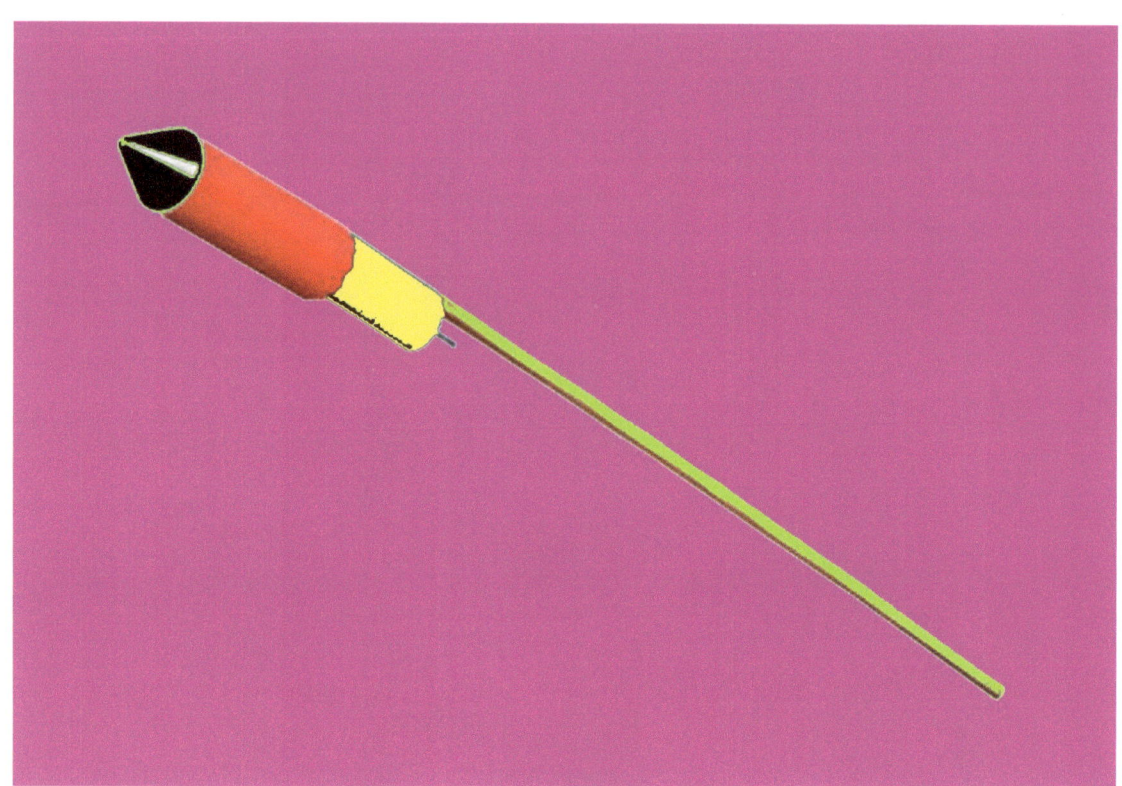
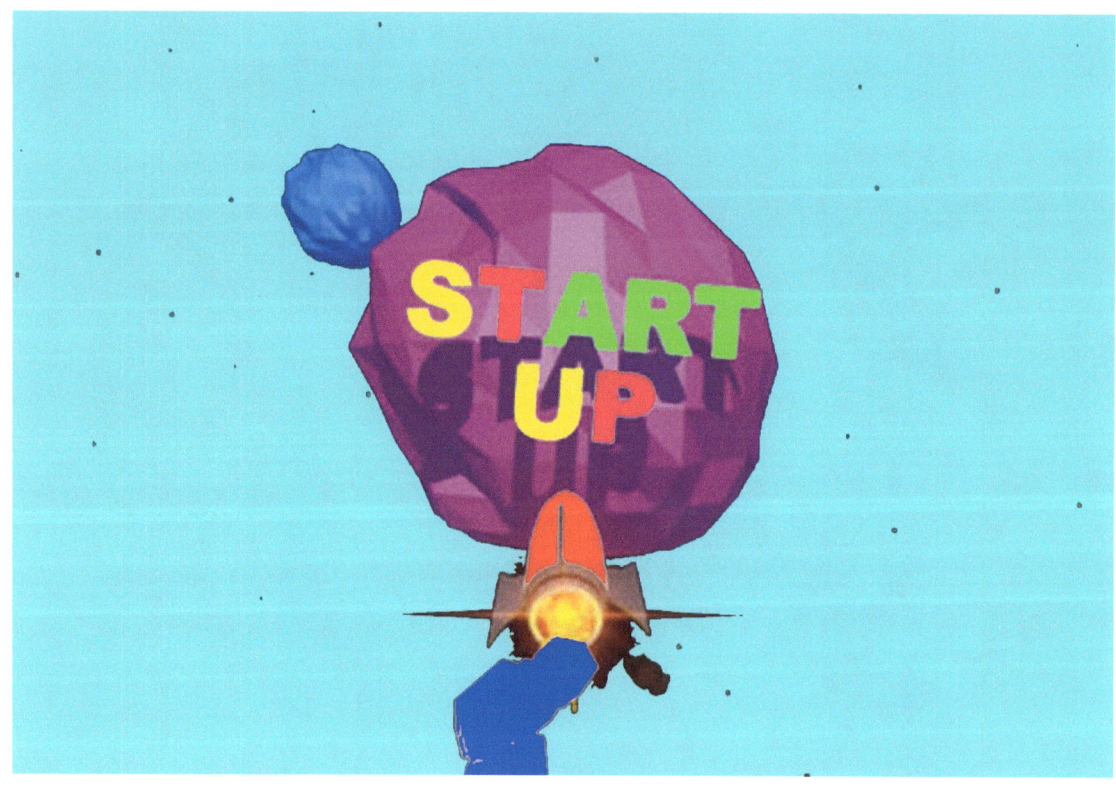

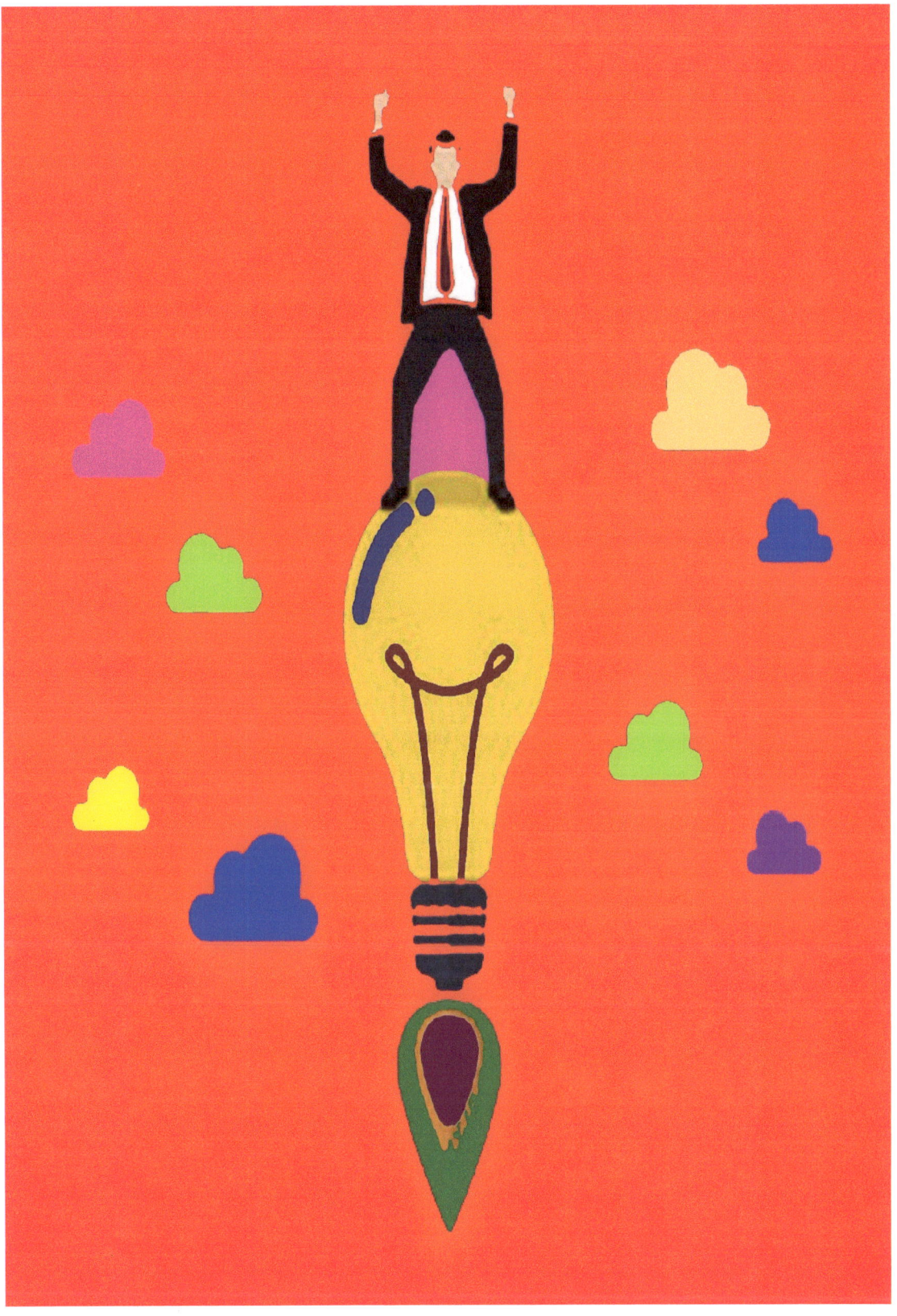

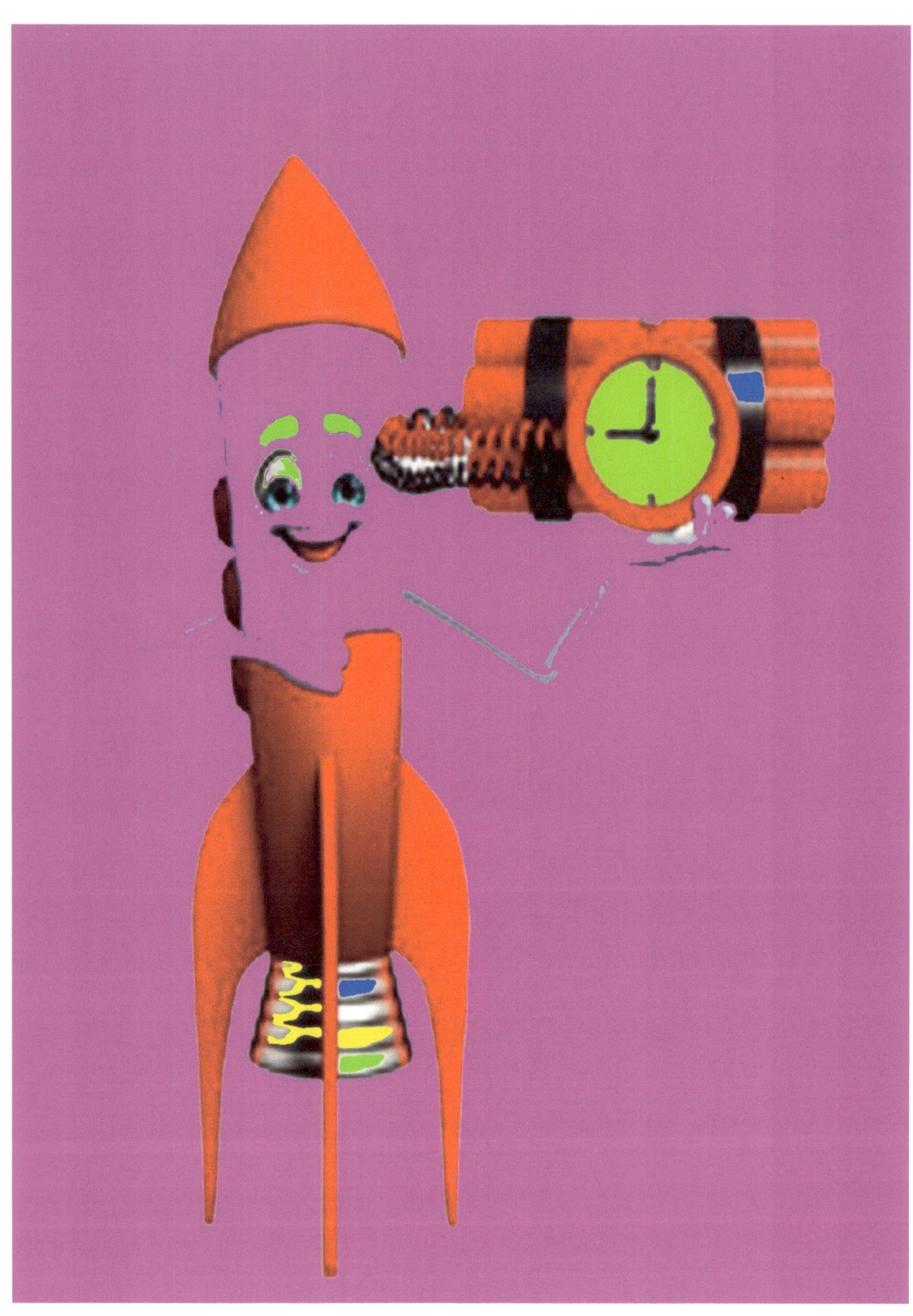

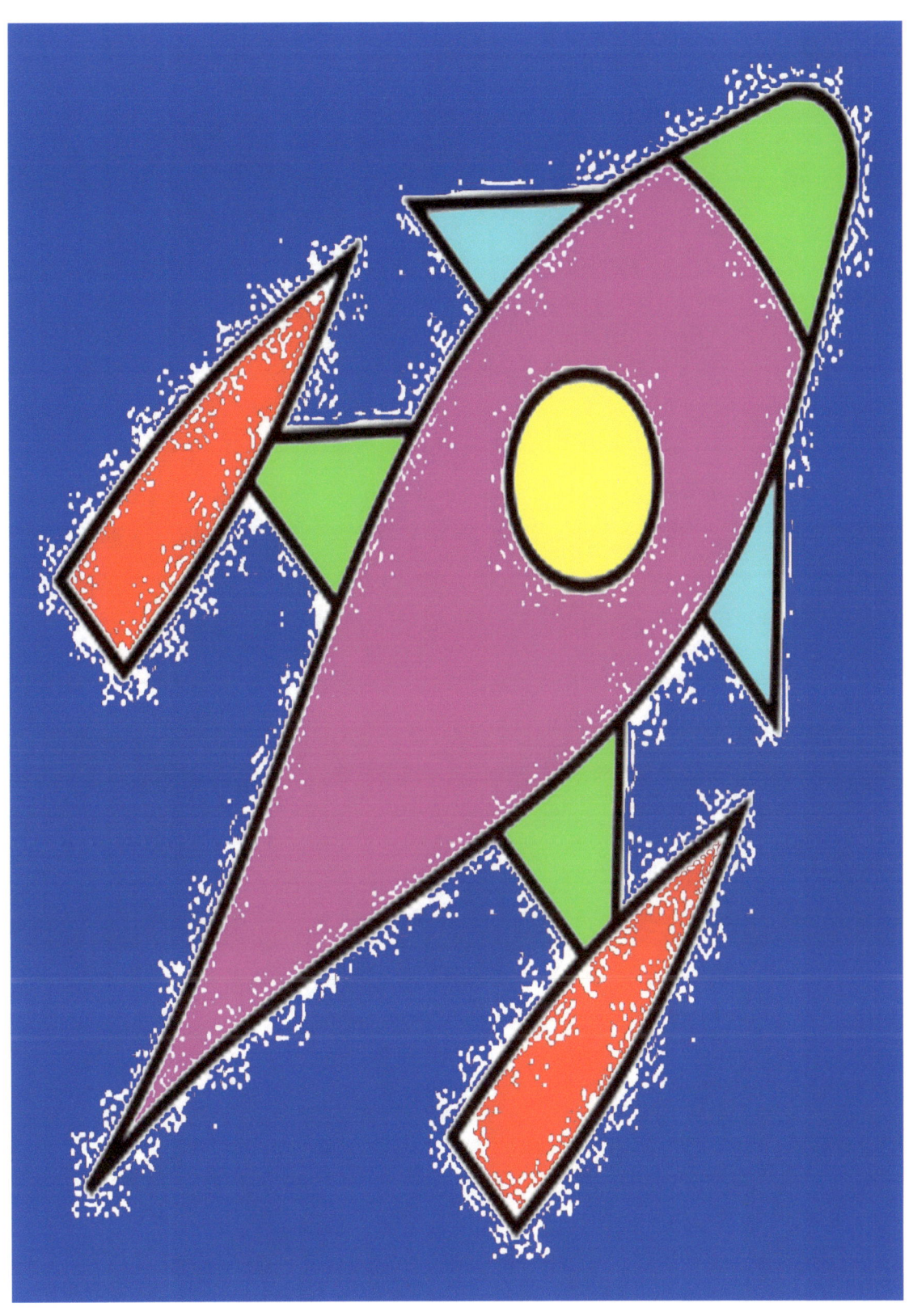

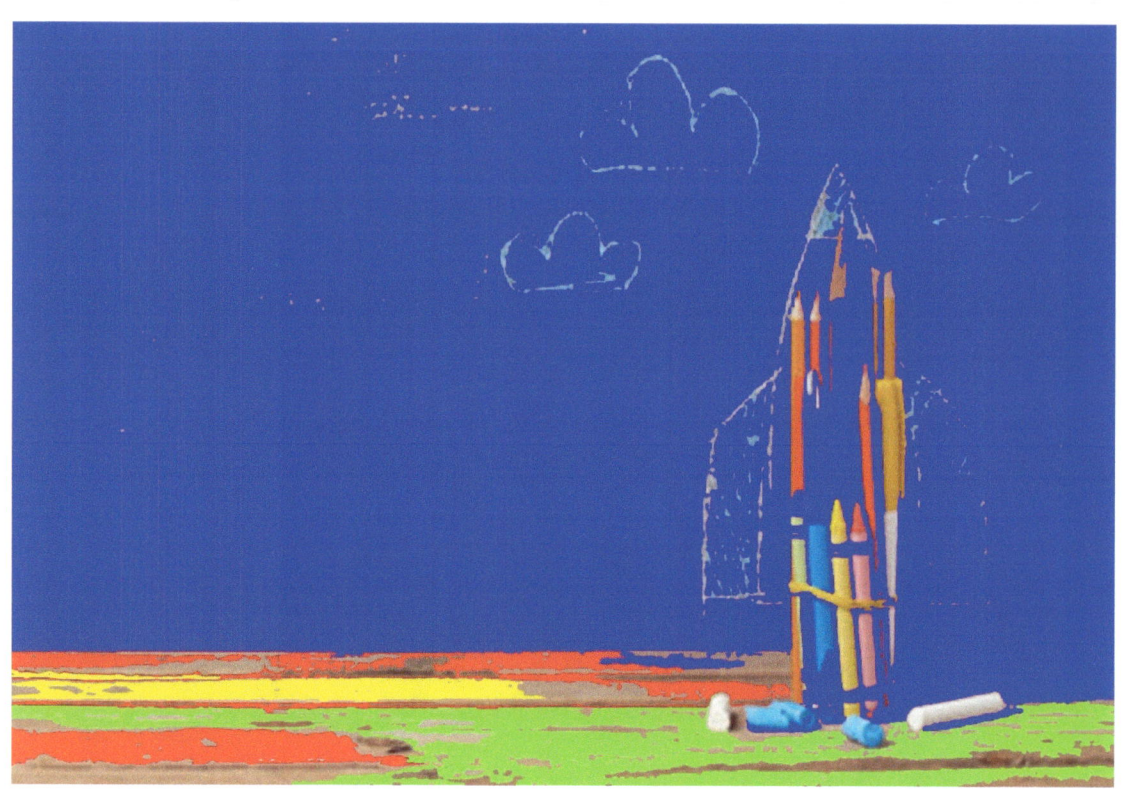

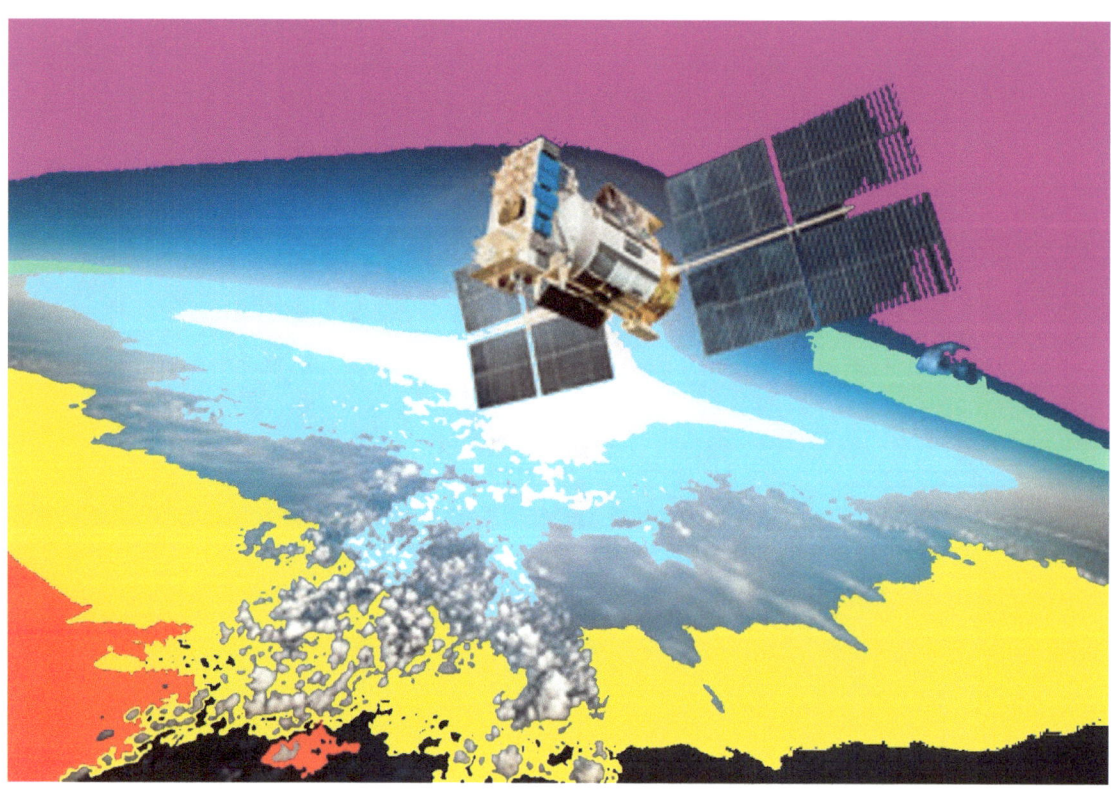

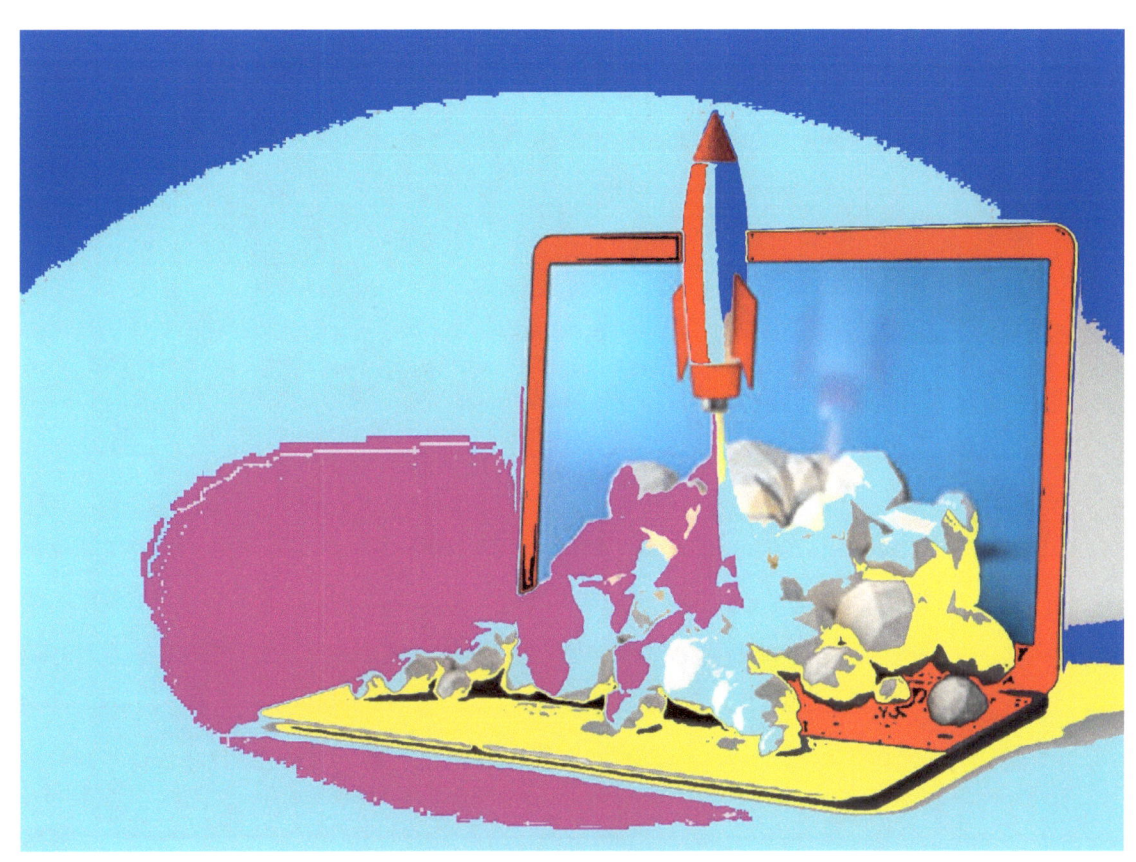

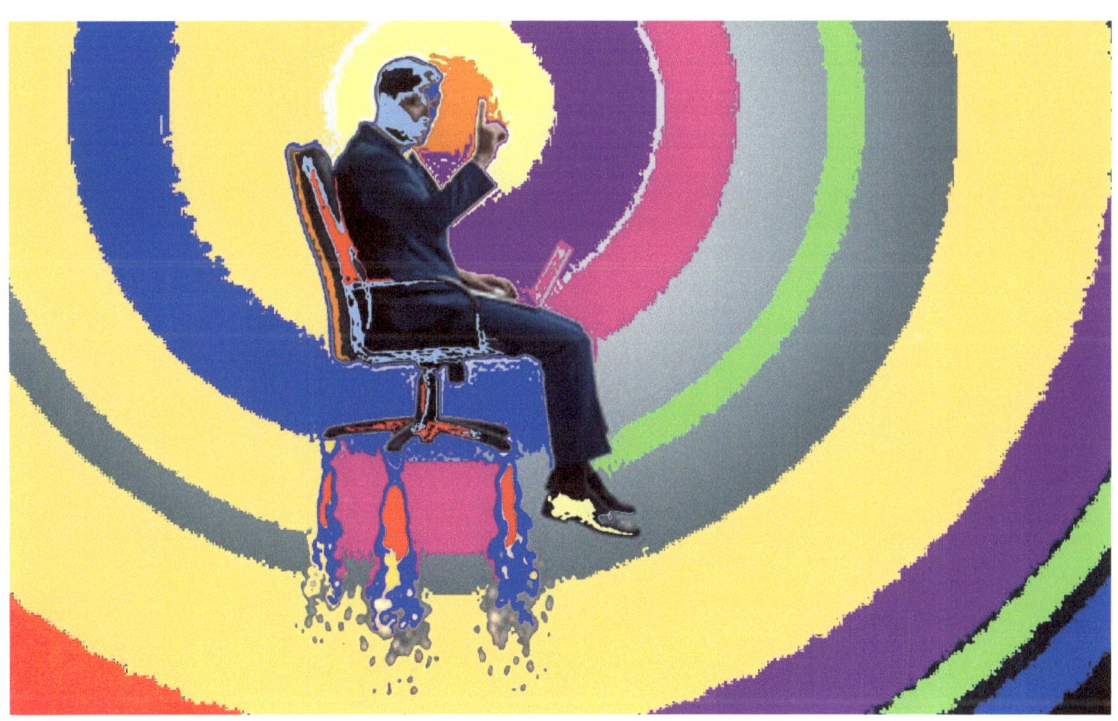

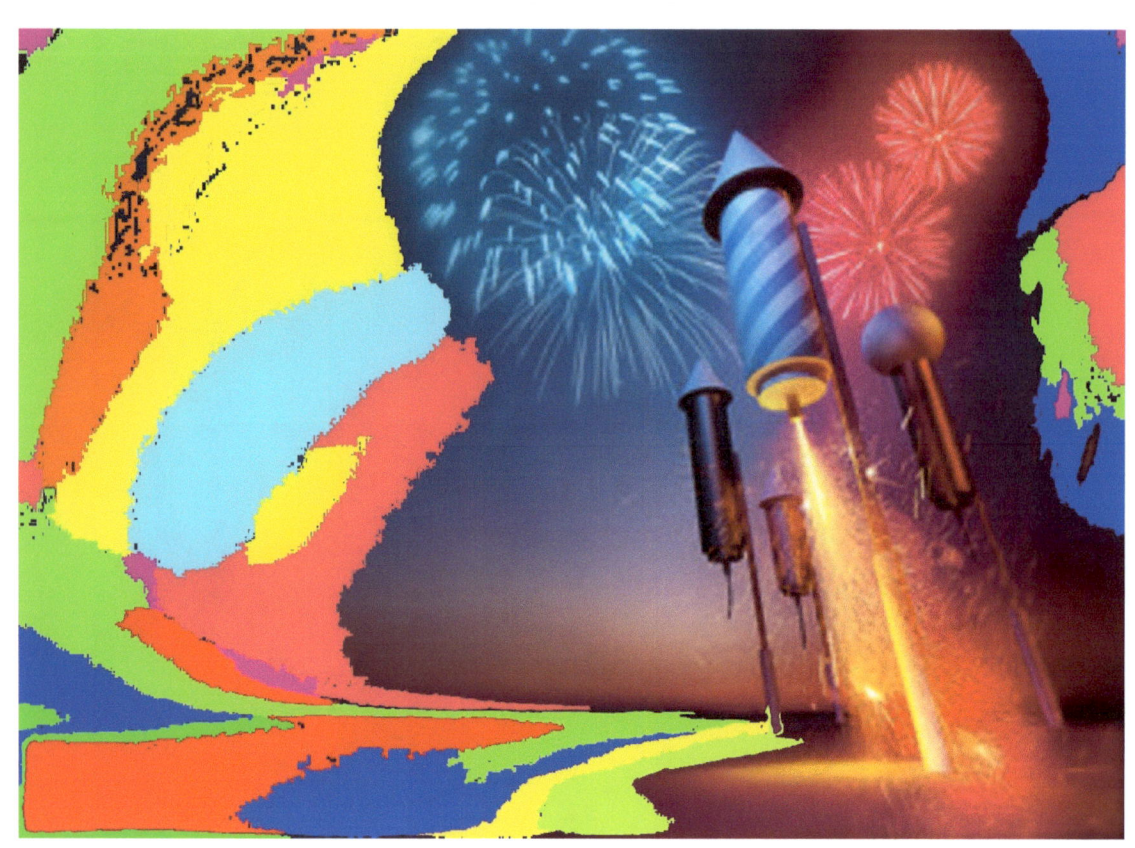

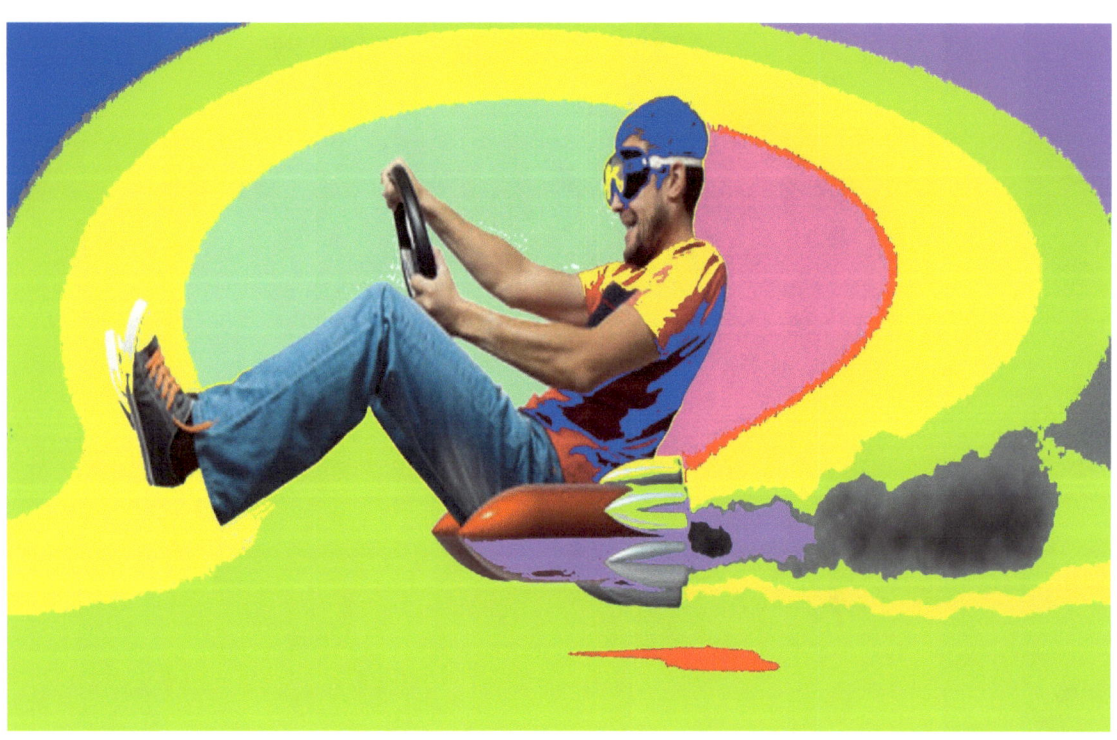

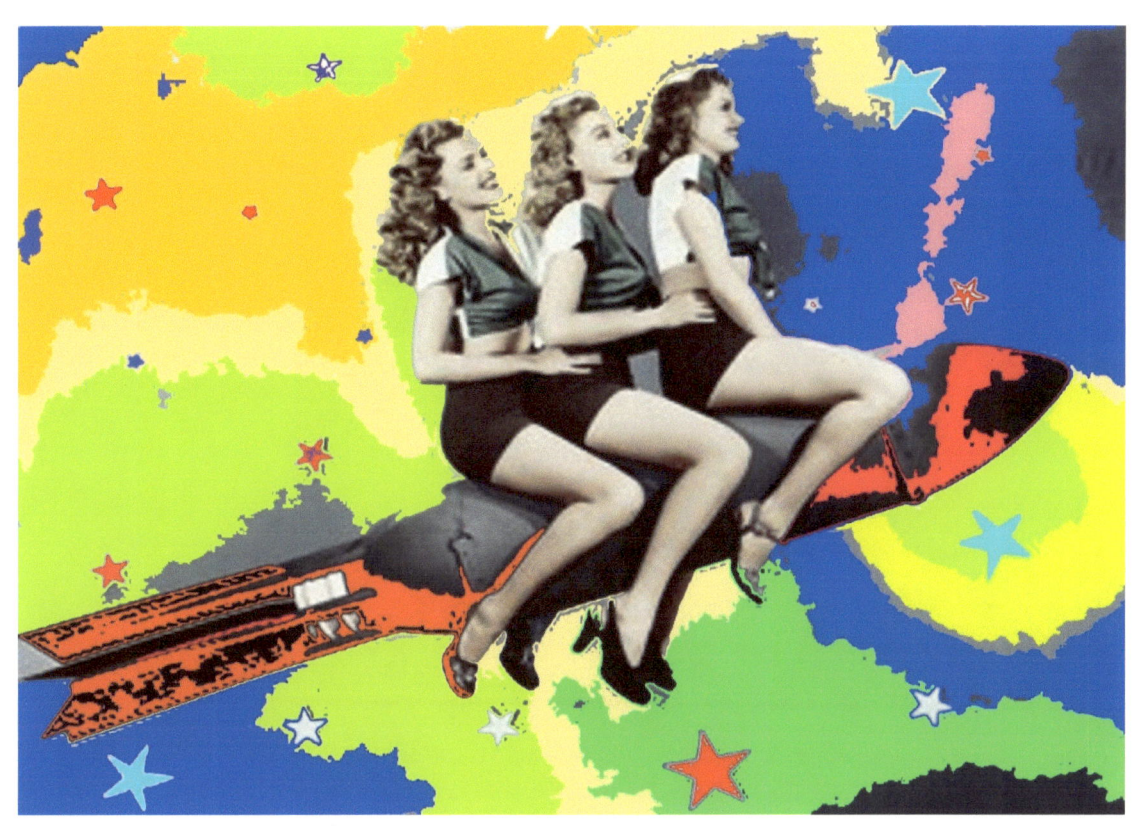

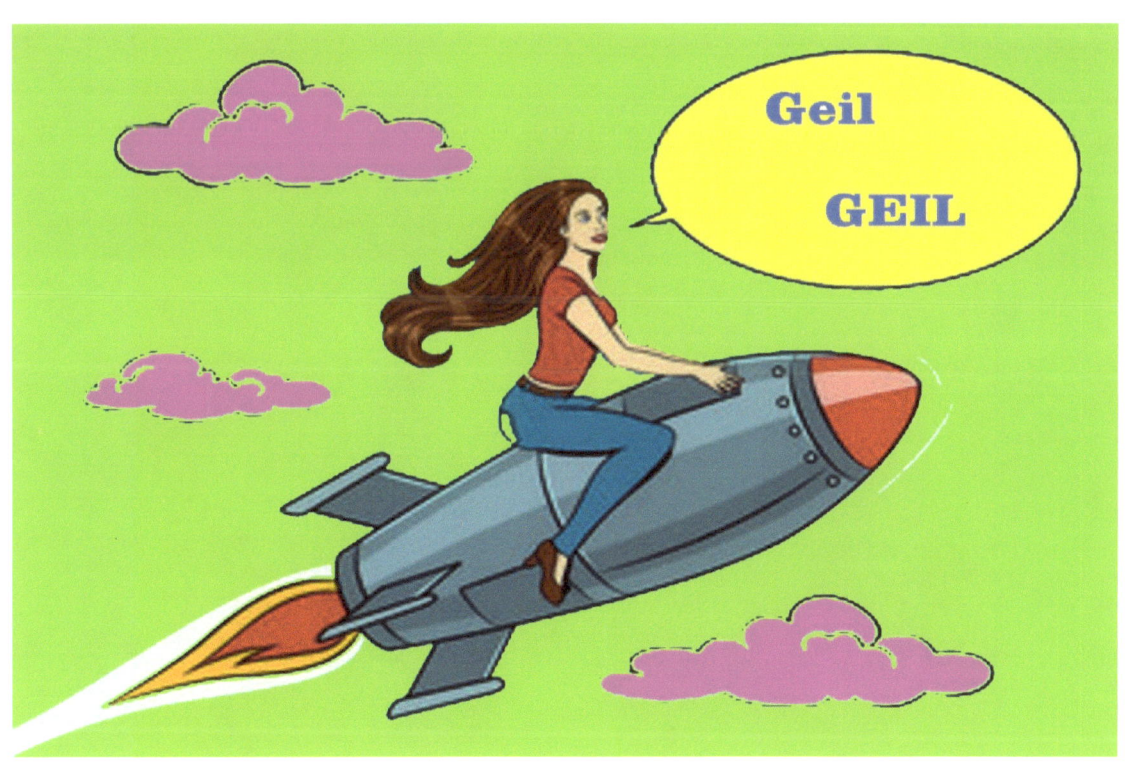

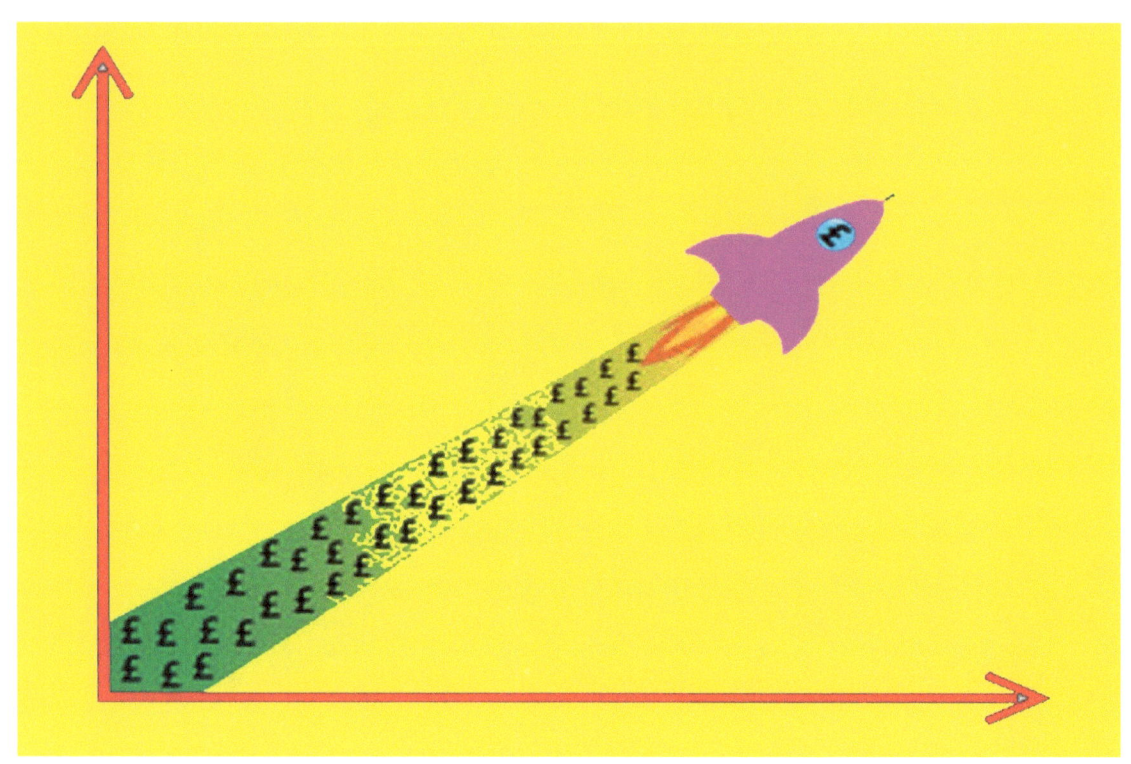

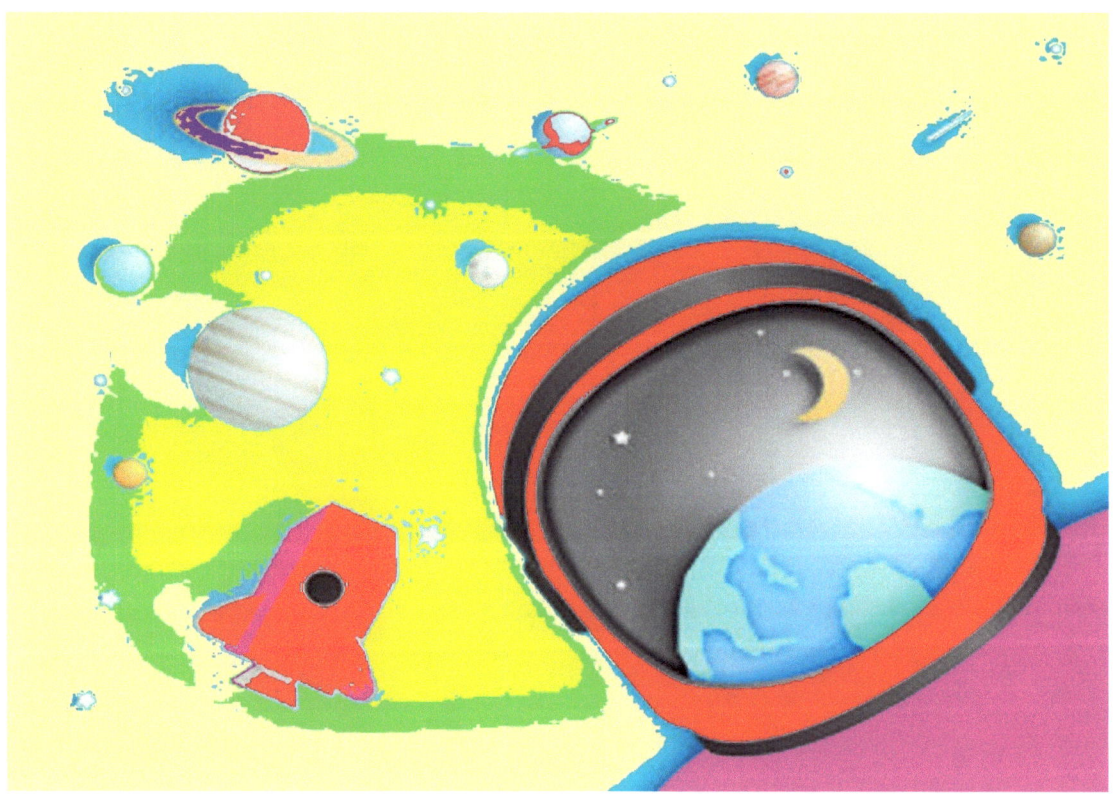

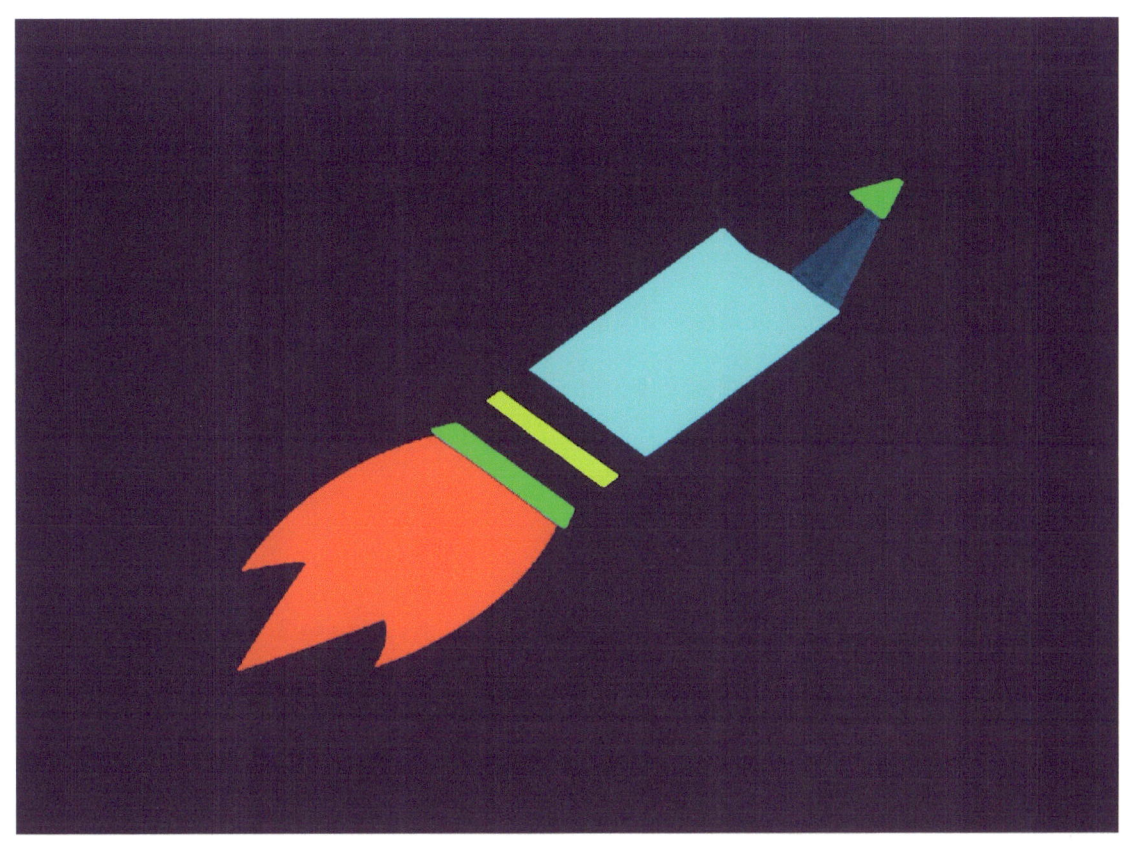
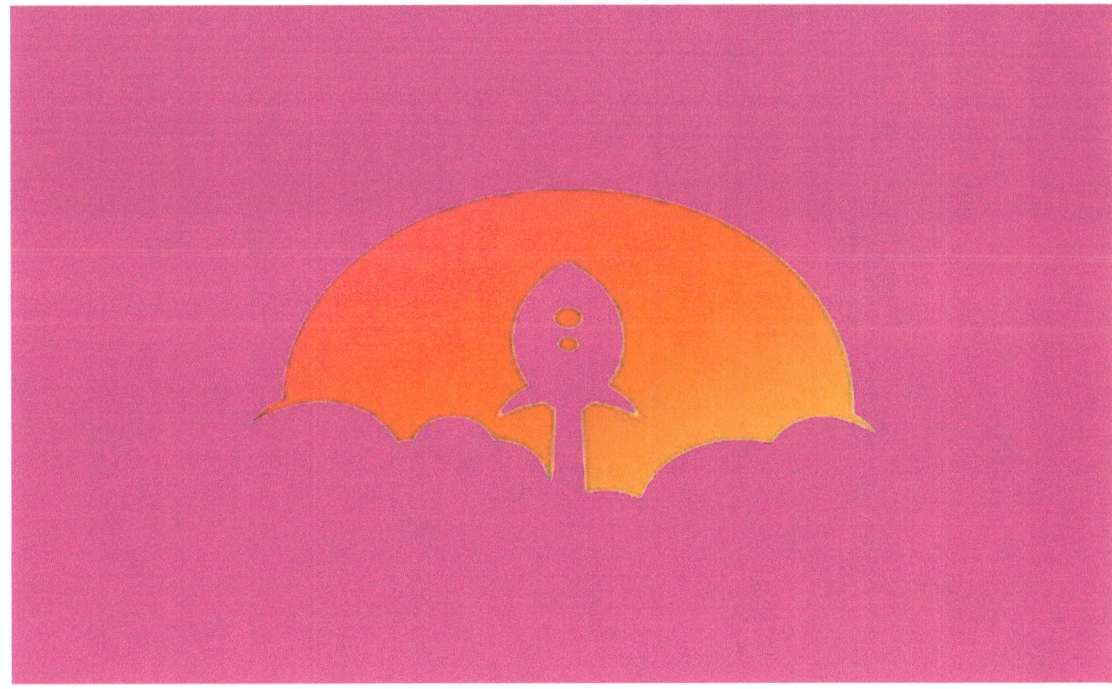

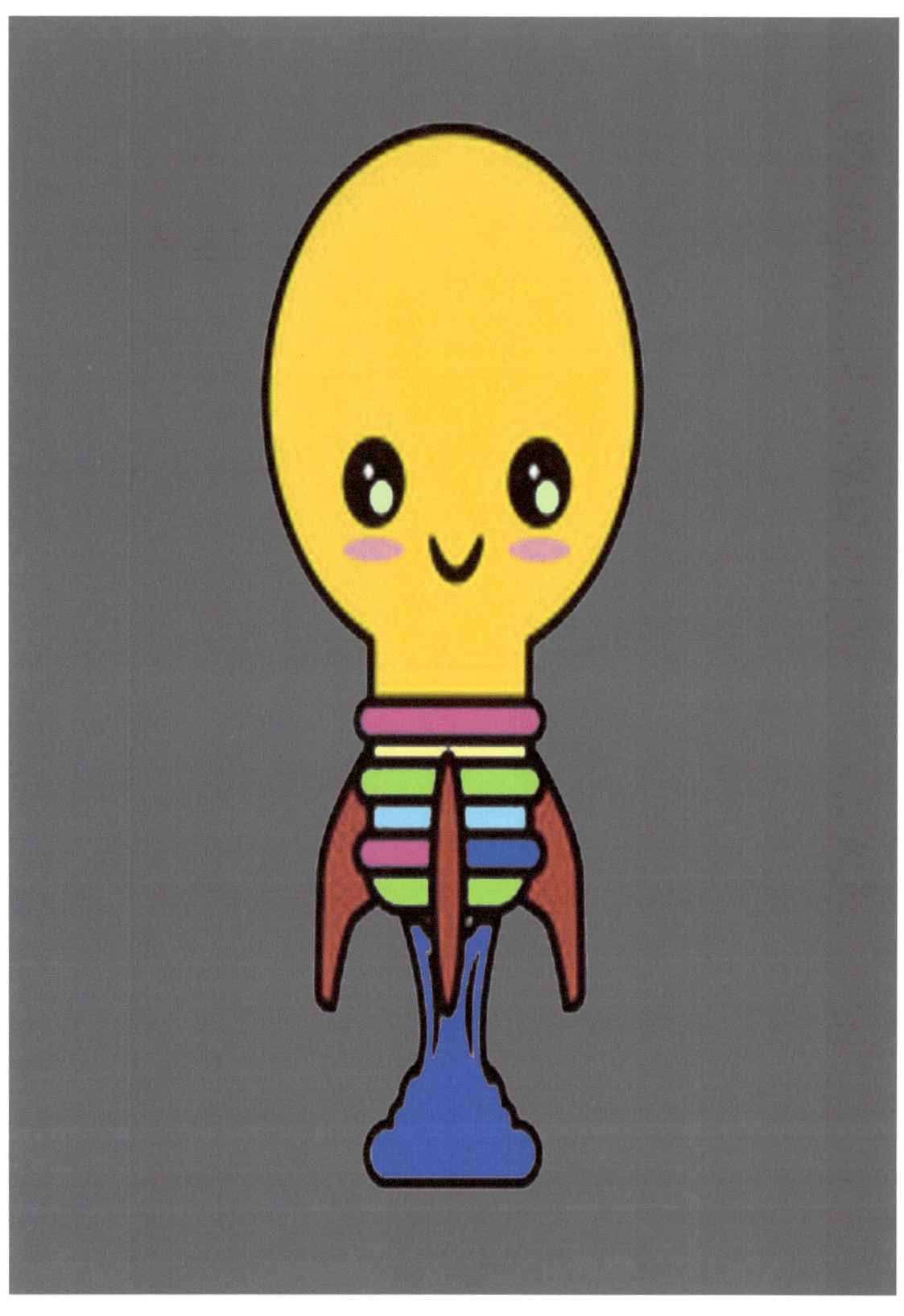

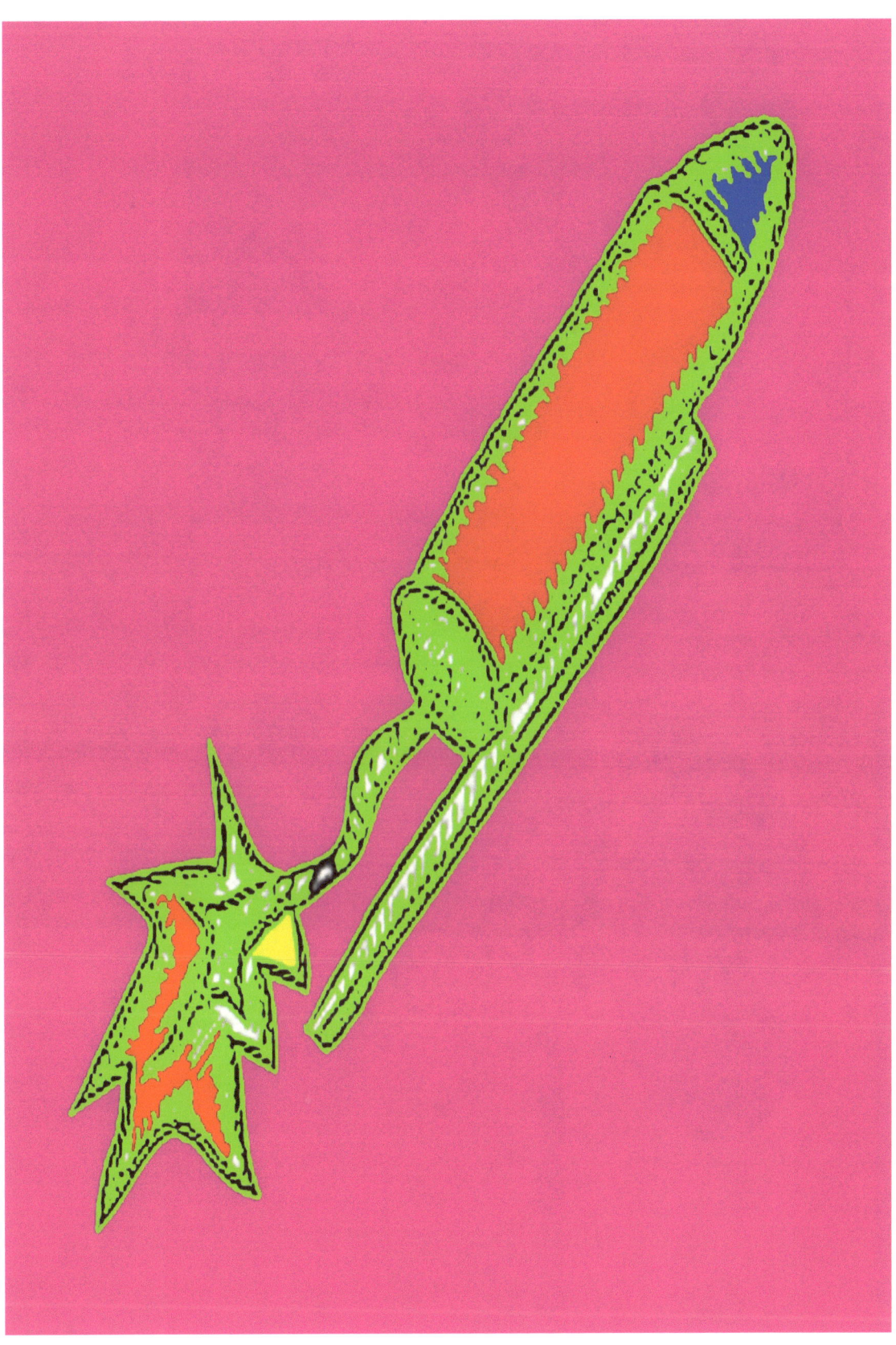

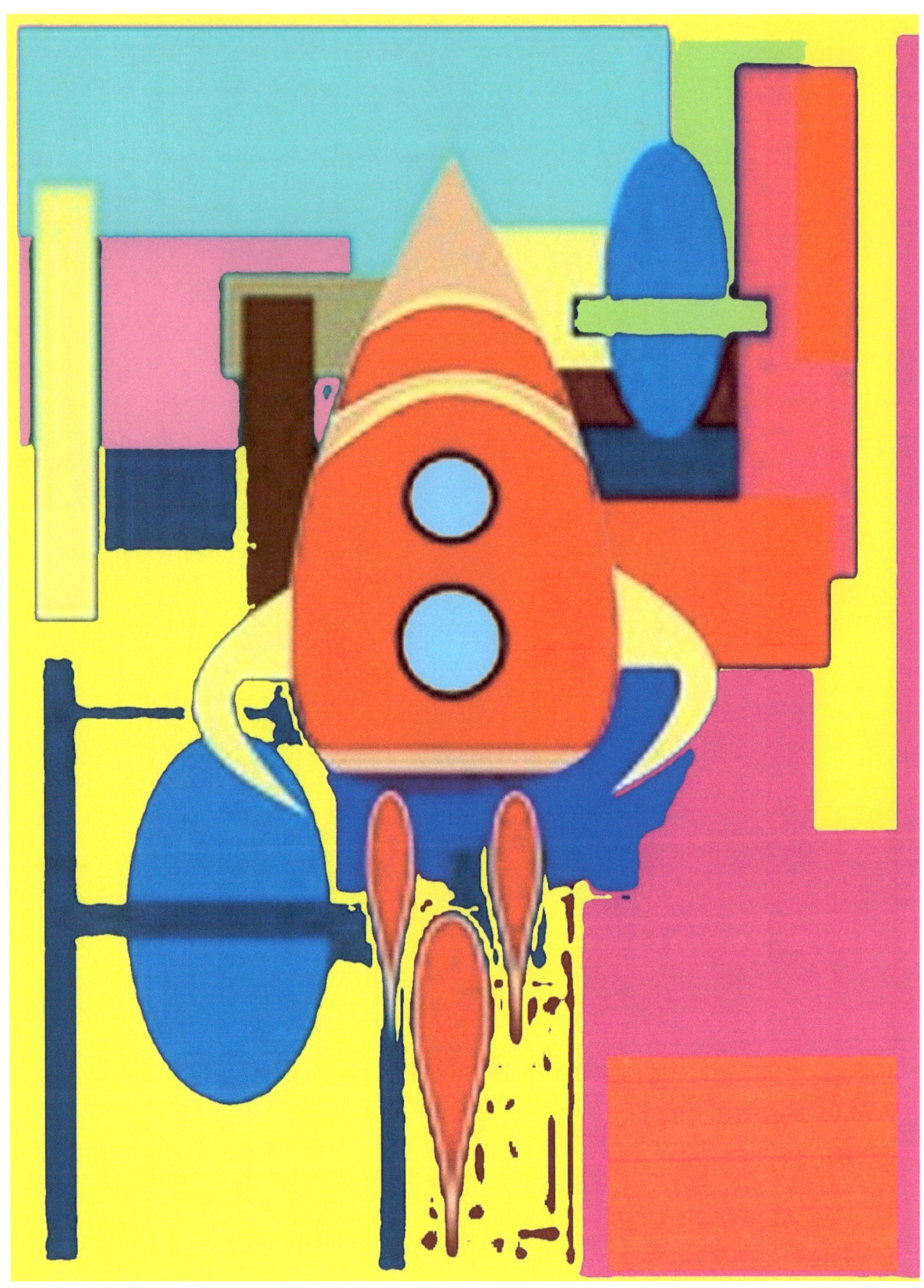

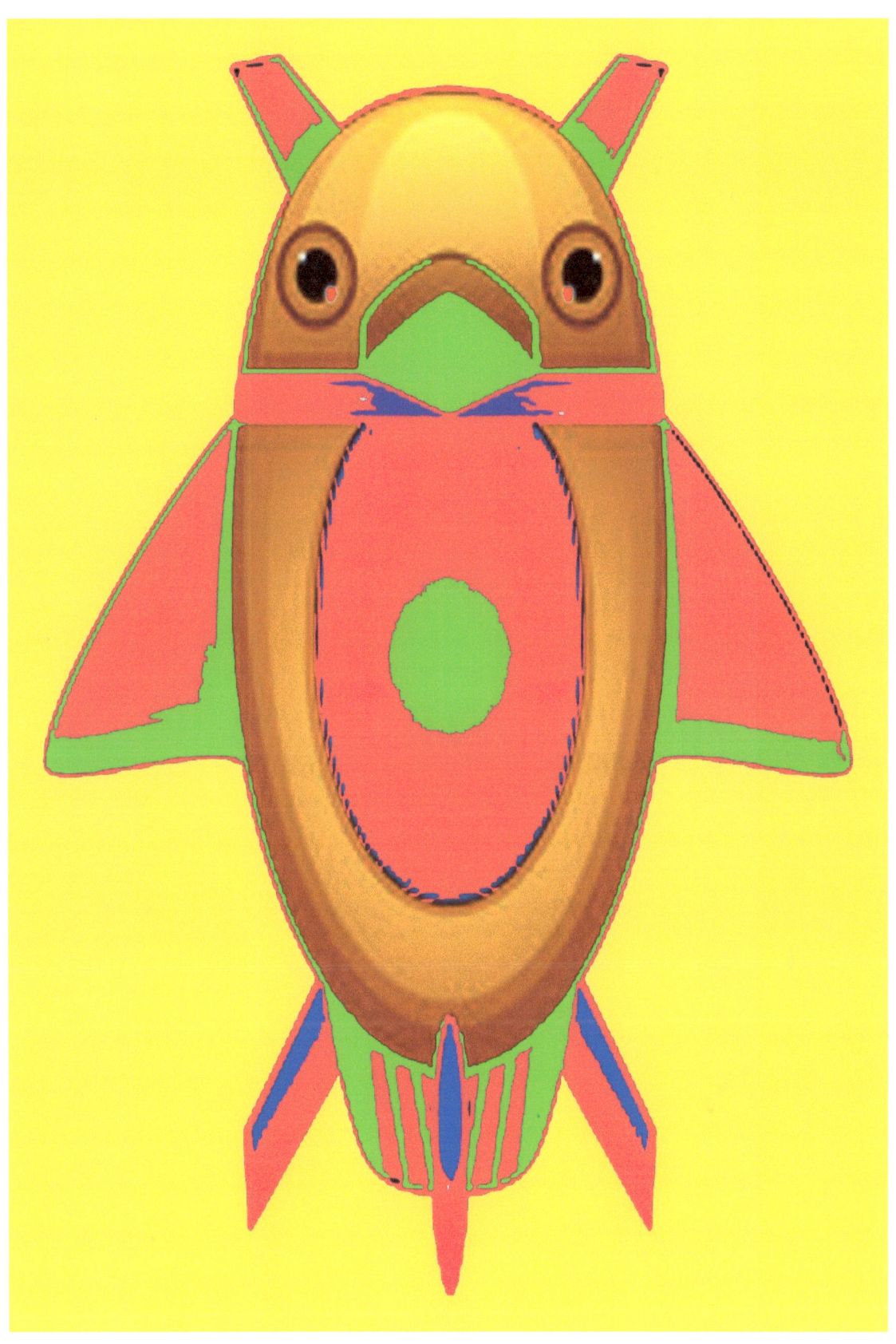

Anhang

Der Bildband Pop Art Raketen ist auch auf folgenden Verkaufskanälen als eBook erhältlich:

Amazon Kindle

Barnes & Noble

Casa del Libro

iBookstore

Kobo/Fnac

Weltbild, Hugendubel, Thalia, buch.de, buecher.de.

Donauland.at, Google Play Books, e-Sentral, Scribd

und einige mehr... .

www.ingramcontent.com/pod-product-compliance
Lightning Source LLC
Chambersburg PA
CBHW041934240526
45473CB00034B/1647